John Berkenhout

A Volume of Letters from Dr. Berkenhout to his Son at the University

John Berkenhout

A Volume of Letters from Dr. Berkenhout to his Son at the University

ISBN/EAN: 9783337106966

Printed in Europe, USA, Canada, Australia, Japan

Cover: Foto ©ninafisch / pixelio.de

More available books at **www.hansebooks.com**

A VOLUME

OF

LETTERS

FROM

Dr. BERKENHOUT

TO HIS

SON AT THE UNIVERSITY.

CAMBRIDGE,

Printed by J. ARCHDEACON Printer to the UNIVERSITY;

For T. CADELL, London.

MDCCXC.

TO THE RIGHT HONORABLE

THOMAS,

LORD VISCOUNT WEYMOUTH,

THIS VOLUME

IS INSCRIBED

BY HIS LORDSHIP'S

FAITHFUL, HUMBLE SERVANT,

THE AUTHOR.

PREFACE.

THESE letters were written partly for the writer's amusement, but principally with the design of introducing the young *fresh*-man, to whom they were addressed, to an early acquaintance with the elements of the sciences he was about to cultivate: they were not designed, in any degree, to supersede, or render less necessary, the instructions of his college-tutors; rather, on the contrary, to facilitate the cultivation, by clearing the surface of its indigenous weeds, and thus preparing the fresh land for the reception of the plough.

Young minds naturally incline to frivolous dissipation; they cannot continue long inactive; it seems therefore necessary to allure them to rational pursuits, before trifling becomes a habit.

A fastidious examiner, will, in these epistles, find sufficient matter for criticism; but, I hope, he will allow me to plead the privilege of that inattention to absolute precision and methodical arrangement, which, in familiar

miliar letters, it were unjuſt, and perhaps improper, to require. The variety of ſub-jects on which I have indulged my ſpeculations, may make the volume appear a *maze*, but, I truſt, *not without a plan*; a plan of which no judgement can be formed from the few pages contained in this volume. The ſubjects are frequently varied, on purpoſe to relieve the attention, and to avoid the formality of a ſyſtematic treatiſe.

I have preſumed, in ſome parts of theſe epiſtles, to cenſure the preſent ſyſtem of education in both Univerſities; but I have alſo acknowledged them, in their preſent ſtate of imperfection, equal to the production of very learned men: neverthelefs, the entire ſyſtem is too obviouſly Gothic to eſcape the ridicule of ſtrangers, who viſit Oxford and Cambridge with the idea, that the *Ecclefia Anglicana* is a *reformed* Church, and that theſe formal ſeminaries are appropriated to the education of nobility, of gentlemen, ſtateſmen, lawyers, phyſicians, and divines.

In the botanical letters, I may be accuſed of pedantry in too frequently *larding the lean earth* with Latin quotations; but the reader muſt not forget the age and recent

ſtudies

ftudies of him to whom they were addreffed, and that nothing fo effectually fixes a new idea in the mind, as attaching it to an old one.

Thofe who, in the perufal of this volume, expect to find amufement, will probably be difappointed: if it prove in any degree, inftructive to young ftudents, the defign of its publication is anfwered.

I muft now beg the reader's indulgence whilft I expoftulate a little with a fraternity of periodical critics, who affume the title of *Analytical Reviewers*, relative to a late publication of mine, entitled *Synopfis of the Natural Hiftory of Britain*, &c. Thefe critics, or rather the individual who did me the honour to review that book, after allowing it fome merit, writes thus — " In the vegetable kingdom, the author juftly acknowledges the affiftance he had from the works of Hudfon, Lightfoot, Curtis, and Withering, moft of whofe plants he has adopted, rather too implicitly, for not one of their errors, even the moft notorious, is corrected."

The accufation may be juft. Poffibly I may have depended too implicitly on what I believed to be fubftantial authority; but furely it was incumbent on the reviewer to

pre-

prevent the propagation of thefe errors, by a fpecific charge. This fort of general criticifm, is, in the higheft degree, illiberal, becaufe it can anfwer no purpofe, fave that of depreciating the book.

In the prefent inftance I was thruft into the *condemned-hole* with four eminent, very eminent, botanifts. Such company might have rendered the dungeon tolerable: but, confidering myfelf as the inftrument of their condemnation, I thought myfelf obliged to juftify them if it were in my power. With this intention, I wrote to the publifher of the *Analytical Review*, requefting, that the writer of the article in queftion would do me the favour, to point out a few of the *notorious* errors, which he had difcovered in the *Synopfis*; errors which, notwithftanding their notoriety, had eluded the obfervation of the other Reviews; errors which, with a view to the greater accuracy of a future edition, I fincerely wifhed to find, but which I had fought for in vain. To this requeft I received no anfwer, either privately, or in any of their fubfequent publications.

L E T-

LETTERS, &c.

LETTER I.

Trumpington, June, 1789.

———— "All the world is a stage,
And all the men and women meerly players:
They have their exits and their entrances,
And one man in his time plays many parts,
His acts being seven ages."————

I NEED not tell you, that these lines begin the admirable speech of *Jaques* in the second act of Shakespear's *As you like it.* These seven ages are, that of the infant, the school-boy, the lover, the soldier, the justice, the pantaloon, and second childhood. This division is poetically just; but it is not generally applicable. The three material *epochas* in the life of a man liberally educat-

A

ed,

ed, are—his admiſſion at a grammar-ſchool, his matriculation at the univerſity, and his departure thence. Theſe three periods, like the three primitive colours, are diſtinctly marked. Shakeſpear's ſeven ages reſemble Sir Iſaac Newton's ſeven priſmatic tincts, four of which are intermediate ſhades, produced by the mixture of the primitive red, blue and yellow.

You, my dear boy, have played your part in the firſt of theſe three acts of the great *drama* of life; and I hope your performance hath been ſuch as to be no diſgrace to the ſtage on which you appeared. In this act you have ſpent eight years of your terreſtrial exiſtence, with all the advantages of a public ſchool. If it be true that, from the age of ten to eighteen, the mind is moſt capable of permanent impreſſions, it were rational to expect that a young gentleman, thus educated, ſhould enter the univerſity poſſeſſed of all the learning neceſſary to conſtitute the foundation of his future ſtudies.

The public ſchools, in this kingdom, profeſſedly, teach nothing but the Greek and Latin languages; and even of theſe, at the expiration of ſeven or eight years, many of the lads have acquired a very ſuperficial

know-

knowledge. They may perhaps be able to conftrue a few pages in the books that have been put into their hands; but are totally loft if you try them in a Greek or Latin author which they have never feen. Would not one be hence naturally led to imagine, that thefe two dead languages are very difficult to learn?—Yet, you have the pleafure to know a young lady to whom Latin and Greek are perfectly familiar; who is likewife an arithmatician, an algebraift, a geometrician; plays the harpficord very finely, fings well, dances in a fuperior ftyle, and is, in fhort, with all her learning, miftrefs of every female accomplifhment.

Now, though I am ready to acknowledge, that this fingular accumulation of acquirements may, in a great degree, be afcribed to a fuperiority of capacity, it demonftrates, neverthelefs, that wonderful effects may be produced by a proper mode of inftruction.

The queftion, why boys learn fo little during feven or eight years continuance at a public fchool? is not difficult of inveftigation. Half that period is confumed in vacations and fingle holidays. It fhould feem therefore, that in our eftimate of the *quantum* of learning, we muft reduce the eight years

to

to four; but this were a falſe eſtimate; for, from theſe four years, we muſt ſubtract the time required to regain what has been abſolutely forgotten and loſt during the ſeveral total ceſſations from learning; and, on a very fair computation, this conſideration will deduct two years from the four: ſo that our eight years are reduced to two; and I will venture to affirm that, under a better ſyſtem, boys might, in two years, be taught all they uſually learn, at any of our public ſchools, in eight.

There is another material impediment in the progreſs of a boy at a public ſchool. I mean the gothic cuſtom of ſuffering the under boys to be the ſervants, the ſlaves, of the upper. Regardleſs of the cruelty of ſubjecting a child to the irrational caprice of a lad of fifteen; regardleſs of the injury he muſt ſuſtain in being conſtantly deprived, by the mandates of his tyrannical maſter, of the ſleep which nature, at that age particularly, requires; regardleſs of that ignominious habit of ſervility which this infamous ſyſtem muſt neceſſarily induce; regardleſs, I ſay, of theſe conſiderations, the menial ſervices to which cuſtom obliges him to attend, leave him little or no time for

appli-

application to his book. What is the confequence?——He is conftantly flogged for
neglect of that which it was not in his
power to execute. There is no appeal. He
dares not complain; *that* would but increafe his fufferings. He fubmits to his
hard fate, and, in refpect to learning, his
four firft years are almoft a total blank.——
But I have filled my paper; Adieu!

LET-

LETTER II.

I MEAN, in some part of this letter, to resume the subject with which I concluded
my last; because I feel myself peculiarly in-
terested in the cause of those defenseless
children, who, whilst they continue *fags* in
a public school, are condemned to greater
hardships than the African slaves whom it
is so much the fashion to commiserate;—
because I wish to keep alive in your memory
those impressions which it may be useful to
future times that you should remember; and
because I would have you perfectly comprehend the reason, why boys from a public
school generally know so little when they
are first sent to the university.

You have too much good sense to con-
strue what I have said into a dissatisfaction
at your ignorance of things which it is impossible you should know. On the contrary, I rather wonder that, under such circumstances, you have acquired so much
knowledge of Latin and Greek: Never-
theless, if you pursue your classical studies, you will soon discover, that you
have

have not yet advanced much farther than the portal to claffical erudition.

The dead languages are nothing more than the external fteps to the temple of literary Fame. A mere pedagogue may conftrue literally every line of Homer, Virgil, Horace, Terence, Cicero, Tacitus, and yet be as ignorant of their real beauties as was Jerediah Buxton of Garrick's. excellence, when, during the performance of the play, he attended only to the number of words fpoken by the actor. The language of the celebrated authors I have mentioned, as language merely, merits, I acknowledge, fome attention; becaufe a perfect acquaintance with the Greek and Latin languages will enable you to underftand and to improve your own. Neverthelefs, if thefe claffical authors poffeffed no merit beyond the mechanical beauty of verbal arrangement and harmony of numbers, they would ill deferve the time and labour they require.

The ftrange cuftom in our public fchools, which conftitutes the under boys fervants to the upper, is fo exceedingly cruel and unjuft, that one cannot help being furprifed at its continuance to the prefent enlightened period of human fociety, when fo many of

the

the abfurdities of our progenitors have been aboliſhed. But the cruelty and injuſtice of this cuſtom are not the only arguments in favour of new regulations. This early ſub-ſerviency and ſubſequent defpotiſm, muſt eventually prove infinitely prejudicial to ſo-ciety. A boy who, from the age of ten to fourteen, hath been compelled to ſubmit to a degree of ſervitude more irkfom and hu-miliating than that of his father's loweſt domeſtic; who is taught, by example, that he muſt ſuffer every ſpecies of impoſition and cruelty without complaint; that his books, his trinkets, and even his apparel, are the property of the boy he calls his maſter: ſuch debaſement, I fay, by thus early bend-ing the mind below the dignity of an Eng-liſh gentleman, muſt infallibly prepare him for ſubmiſſions inimical to the conſtitution of his country.—-- He gradually rifes to the upper ſchool. He then becomes a tyrant in his turn, and theſe habits of tamely ſub-mitting to the mandates of his ſuperiors, and of capricioufly tyrannizing over thofe beneath him, can hardly fail to form a truly deteſt-able charaćter. But it were unjuſt hence to infer, that every gentleman educated at our great public ſchools is a compound of

ſlave

flave and tyrant.   There are many examples
of the contrary.

The late King of Pruffia, without any advantage of education, was a great General,
a confummate Politician, an acute Philofopher, a good Poet and a polite Scholar, even
without any knowledge of the dead languages.   In like manner, our immortal Shakefpear, without education, was doubtlefs the
firft of all dramatic poets.   It appears therefore, that the characters of men are not in-
variably caft in the mould of education,
and that even a total want of it cannot prevent fuperior intellects from rifing above
the common level of mankind.   Of this
truth there cannot be a more fingular example than the prefent father of the Medical faculty in the Univerfity of Edinburgh.
Dr. Cullen I have always regarded as one of
thofe rare beings, whofe intuitive rays of
underftanding penetrate the clouds of time-
fanctioned erroneous opinions, even without
the labour of formal inveftigation.

But thefe are fingular examples.   Mankind, in general, are the creatures of tuition
and habit; we may therefore fairly conclude,
that a mixture of fervility and imperiouf-
nefs will generally mark the character of
young

young gentlemen educated at Weſtminſter, Eton or the Charter Houſe; and hence it is ſurely incumbent on every pupil of theſe ſchools, carefully to examine his acquired propenſities, and to correct the evil before habit ſhall have rendered it an indelible feature is his character. Machiavel, the famous, the infamous, Italian politician, depended ſo much on the effect of cuſtom, that he adviſes princes who wiſh to remove their opponents by aſſaſſination, to employ none but fellows whoſe hands are already ſtained with blood. He reaſoned from a juſt knowledge of mankind. In ſuffering children to torture flies, we ſow the ſeeds of cruelty, which, like the paraſitical Ivy, will grow up with the ſaplen and cling to every branch.

You will in the courſe of your ſtudies at the univerſity neceſſarily become acquainted with *Locke's Eſſay on Human Underſtanding*. He was of opinion that we are born without ideas, and conſequently that all ideas are impreſſions on the brain from external objects, received and communicated by our ſenſes. If this be true, we are entirely the creatures of education, and the difference of character between one boy and another,

edu-

educated at the fame fchool, muft depend on their different capacity, or aptitude to receive and retain the fame impreffions. Habits, therefore, of fervility and fucceffive tyranny, will contaminate the difpofition of one youth more than another; but every young gentleman emerging from a public fchool, fhould examine his difpofition with miftruft. "Probably (he fhould fay to himfelf) from my early habits of fervility, I am too much inclined to kneel to my fuperiors; and, in confequence of my late defpotic command, I am difpofed to tyrannize over my dependents; I am pofitive in my opinions, and too impatient of contradiction."

You have read, I dare fay, that when Socrates was interrogated concerning his vaft knowledge, he anfwered that *the chief of what he knew was that he knew nothing.* Sir Ifaac Newton thought fo humbly of his fuperior abilities, that he conftantly afcribed his wonderful difcoveries folely to application, which he faid, was in every man's power. The great Locke entitled his admirable *Treatife on Human Underftanding,* merely *an Effay.* From thefe examples, we may rationally conclude, that arrogance makes no part of the character of a great

man;

man; that, in purfuit of knowledge, *alps on alps arife* before us; that the profpect extends in proportion to our elevation; and that when we have gained the fummit of the mountain, the expanfe of fcience is bounded only by the univerfe.

From this elevation, let us now look back upon yon fpruce young gentleman at the bottom of the hill. He has juft left the fchool which you fee at a diftance in the valley. The moment he had fhook hands with his fchoolfellows, he runs into a barber's fhop, and, with a manly importance, fits down to have his *no-beard* fhaved off, and his graceful ringlets, bound ridgedly up in the form of a carrot, powdered and perfumed; his *leathers* up to his ribs, blue filk ftockings, harnefs buckles and a club in his hand, he begins his journey towards the temple of Fame. He miftakes the mountain before him for a fmooth plane, and, perfectly confident in his acquired *momentum*, he expects to roll on with the rapidity and eafe of a Phaeton on the turf. Alas! he ftumbles at the firft ftep. He meets, as he afcends, with difficulties which he did not expect. His refolution fails. He fickens at the profpect before him, and never advances

a fina single step farther. So ends the progress of far the greatest number of students at the university. Indolence, evil habits, and fashionable dissipation, are the universal impediments to useful knowledge and rational acquirements. That you may profit by the contemplation of this picture, is the ardent wish of, dear Charles,

Your, &c.

LETTER III.

IN my two former letters I have endeavoured to find a reason, why boys, educated at any of our public schools, come to
the university totally ignorant of every
thing, except a little Greek and Latin: and
that I might let them down as gently as I
possibly could, I have, and I think justly,
ascribed their want of knowledge to a gothic
system of Instruction. The dead languages
are doubtless the foundation of modern erudition; but certainly more, much more
might be acquired in the course of seven or
eight years, if more than half that time
were not sacrificed to custom. It is indeed
very extraordinary that, in discarding the
absurdities of the Romish creed and religious ceremonies, we should have retained
so much of the ancient mode of education,
both in our schools and universities.

Perhaps I am not justifiable in exciting
in you an unfavourable idea of the mode of
education established in the university of
which you are become a member. But I
now start the subject, to prevent your sud-
denly

denly drinking the poiſon of diſguſt before you are provided with an antidote.

In the univerſity of Cambridge, though claſſical learning be not neglected, yet mathematical ſtudies are particularly enforced. A young gentleman intended for no profeſſion, who ſpends a few years at the univerſity only becauſe he is yet too young to make the tour of Europe, cannot eaſily be perſuaded that the moſt perfect knowledge of Euclid's Elements can ever be of any uſe to him: he therefore applies reluctantly, or not at all, to the ſtudy of a ſcience from which he can receive no advantage. Thoſe who are deſigned for Law, Phyſic or Divinity, are equally at a loſs to apply mathematics to their ſeveral profeſſions. Very true: mathematical knowledge is not immediately applicable to Law, Phyſic or Divinity; neverthelefs it is indirectly connected with, and fundamental to, all ſcience. It neceſſarily induces a habit of reaſoning juſtly; it accuſtoms the mind to rational inveſtigation and intenſe thinking. Now, intenſe thinking, without which you muſt always remain on the ſurface of knowledge, is, to common minds, an occaſional and irkſome exertion; but, to a mathematician

it

it is habitual and eafy: in all fubjects of difficulty therefore, a mathematician has an evident advantage; his conceptions will be more diftinct; his deductions more accurate, and his conclufions confequently more juft.

There is yet another very ftrong recommendation to mathematical ftudies. I mean amufement. Exclufive of their univerfal utility, you will find them infinitely entertaining. Few pleafures are equal to that of folving a difficult problem. Comply therefore with the habits of the univerfity; apply yourfelf ardently to the rudiments of mathematical knowledge, and look forward with confidence to the reward of your labour. But, before you proceed, I muft caution you againft that fatal *cui bono?* which being a queftion not always eafily anfwered, is often confidered as an *argumentum crucis* againft the application to a fcience the utility of which is not immediately obvious. In this turbulent fea of human life, we fee but a very few leagues before us. Sagacity and experience, our two beft telefcopes, difcover no land a-head; but that is no proof that we may not, before the next glafs, fall in with an ifland or continent. Univerfal knowledge is far beyond the reach of human

man

man capacity; but fcience is the falutary food of the human foul, and fhould therefore be cultivated for its own fake, totally legardlefs of its ufeful application. We are diftinguifhed from the brute creation only in proportion to our mental acquirements, and furely every intelligent being would wifh to remove himfelf as far as poffible from the brute creation.

Young men are naturally vain and pofitive; dictatorial and dogmatical in their opinions, becaufe they have not learnt to reafon juftly, and becaufe they are unacquainted with the arguments by which they might be refuted: and it frequently happens that they are confirmed in their errors by the contemptuous filence of Learning and Experience. I fpeak of young men in general. You have certainly too much penetration not to perceive the abfurdity of juvenile arrogance. I dwell upon this fubject, becaufe this arrogance is an infuperable obftacle to all knowledge.

A young man, fortunately infpired with an enthufiaftic defire of knowledge, will begin by a fcrupulous inveftigation of the nature and degree of the learning which he brings to the univerfity. Probably he will

B .

dif-

difcover that he knows lefs, even of vulgar arithmetic, than a fhopkeeper's apprentice, and has lefs knowledge of the world than a gentleman's *Valet de Chambre*. This may poffibly be confidered as a very humiliating reflexion to a fpruce young academician; it is true neverthelefs; and it is not only true, but the confcioufnefs of it is the only pedeftal to his future pillar of Fame. He that does not build upon humility will never rife to diftinction. Arrogance is difgufting even in thofe who have moft reafon to be proud; what then muft it not be in thofe who have no pretenfion to eminence? Be not therefore afhamed to fay with Socrates, *All I know is that I know nothing.*

What is human knowledge? What are its objects? They are Arts or Sciences. Arts I confider as manual, mechanical, operations: they are corporal attainments. Sciences, on the contrary, are more immediately objects of the mind. You will find fome difficulty in drawing a ftraight line between them, becaufe moft arts require fome degree of Science: neverthelefs, by the help of an example or two, we fhall poffibly be able to feperate the two ideas, fo as to keep them tollerably diftinct.

Mufic,

Mufic, for example, is an *art*, a liberal art. Cramer in executing a difficult *concerto*, whether of his own compofition or not, is a wonderful *artift*; but refpecting his compofitions, or his cadences, when really extemporaneous, or invented, he ranks with men of fcience. In like manner, a painter, who does nothing more than copy objects before him, is a mere artift: he is a man of fcience only in proportion to his difplay of his knowledge of Nature. A poet may alfo be confidered as a mere artift, when his fole merit is the accuracy of his verfification.

When you have leifure to confult the writings of philofophers, particularly Ariftotle and his followers, you will find that they have fo perplexed themfelves in their difinition of Arts and Sciences, as to render it impoffible to diftinguifh one from the other. The difinition of Arts, which I have given you above, may be, ftrictly, applicable to mechanical Arts only: this however, is fufficient for our prefent purpofe.

I am, dear Charles, &c.

 L E T-

L E T T E R IV.

I CONCLUDED my laſt letter with a conciſe diſcremination of Arts and Science, which together comprehend the objeĉts of human intelligence, and conſequently the objeĉts of your future application. The former are, at preſent, entirely out of the queſtion. Let us therefore take a general view of the latter.

The Sciences, with which you have at this time any concern, are Arithmetic, Geometry, Logic, Rhetoric, Morality, and Revelation, as a branch of Theology. To theſe will be added, a continuation of your Claſſical ſtudies, with ſome attention to Hiſtory. Of theſe ſciences, you are neceſſarily totally ignorant. You have read, or rather conſtrued, a few detached ſcraps of ancient hiſtory; but that was ſolely with regard to the language in which they were written. As to modern hiſtory, and the manners and improvements of different nations in modern times, you have been entirely precluded by your age and ſituation. From theſe conſiderations it neceſſarily follows, that a boy, a young

gentle-

gentleman, if you rather prefer that denomination, immediately emerging from fchool,
is in truth, and without any reflexion on
his abilities, as I have already obferved in a
former letter, a very ignorant perfonage.
He is ignorant of the world, confequently
embarraffed in his deportment, and totally
unacquainted even with the principles of
any fcience whatfoever.

What then muft we think of thofe young
gentlemen, and fuch young gentlemen are
not very uncommon fpectacles, who, with
all thefe imperfections, inconfiderately dafh
their opinions on all fubjects, in the prefence of Learning and Experience? They
are heard with compaffion, and they retire
uninformed.

Are we then, you will afk, to act the part
of mutes?—No: not abfolutely; but a
young ftripling who talks, only becaufe he
thinks he ought not to be filent, had much
better hold his tongue. If he prefume to
take the lead in converfation, he muft infallibly expofe himfelf; becaufe, like a poor
prodigal, he is extravagant without a fund;
and, like an ignorant pilot, he runs aground
before he has difcovered the coaft. If he
venture to give his opinion on politics, the

 greateft

greateſt favour the company can do him is to ſeem to attend to ſomething elſe. If he preſume to decide on the merit of a book, a ſermon, a play, or an actor, it is at leaſt ten to one againſt him, that he is wrong; becauſe a rational determination on theſe ſubjects requires a degree of knowledge to which a ſchool boy can have no pretenſions. If he think proper to entertain the company with a *good ſtory*, it is moſt probably, though new to himſelf and his *quondam* companions, a ſtale joke to many perſons preſent, and poſſibly the wit of a jeſt-book. —As to wit, in general, it is a plaything ſo very like an edged tool, that it is impoſſile a boy ſhould meddle with it without cutting his fingers. But, beſides the danger, there is another reaſon ſufficient to deter a young man from attempting to be witty. I mean the difficulty of immediately diſtinguiſhing real from falſe wit. The firſt may produce ſome degree of applauſe: the latter, nothing better than a ſneer. Every unſucceſsful attempt to be witty, recoils, like an over-loaded gun; overturns the author, and expoſes him ſprawling to the deriſion of his companions.

In what I have written concerning the general

neral ignorance of Weftminfter, Eton, and Charter-houfe fchool boys, I attribute that ignorance neither to the lads nor to their maf-ters; but partly to the indolence of men in power, and partly to an apprehenfion of the confequences of reformation. We like reformation well enough, whilft, with the reins in our hands, we can ftop it when we pleafe; but we are fearful of Reformation run mad. In reading Swift's *Tale of a Tub*, you will learn that it is not an eafy opera-tion to ftrip a garment of its fuperfluous ornaments, without tearing the cloth. This is an argument againft inconfiderate, irra-tional reformation; but, if it be admitted as an argument againft reformation in ge-neral, it proves too much. If the great re-former Luther had been deterred by fuch arguments, all Europe would ftill have groaned under the ecclefiaftical tyranny of a fovereign Pontif. But I have infenfibly wandered from my fubject.

I do not mean to infinuate that a young gentleman, on his firft admiffion at the Univerfity, when accidentally in the com-pany of his fuperiors, fhould be precluded from taking part in the converfation; but, be his natural abilities ever fo great, he

 fhould,

fhould, on no occafion, prefume to take the lead. His opinions, when afked, fhould be delivered with diffidence, and in a manner evidently expreffing his defire of better information: and this, not only becaufe fuch deportment is moft becoming his fituation; but becaufe it is the only means by which he can expect to improve by the converfation of men of fuperior knowledge. Men of fcience feel a pleafure in communicating their knowledge to young minds properly difpofed for inftruction; but juvenile arrogance, like the moth which is now wheeling round my candle, in the moment that it finges it wings, puts out the light. Nothing fo effectually filences a man of letters as the modifh tittle-tattle, or decifive opinions of a young *Etourdie*.

That *man* is naturally a vain animal, appears from his being moft vain whilft neareft a ftate of nature; that is, before a little education has opened to his view the expanded profpect of human knowledge; before he is convinced, by experience, that error is interwoven with human nature. This vanity is indeed fo natural a vice, that no habit is more difficultly acquired than that of acknowledging our errors; and yet this habit

bit

bit is the beſt feature in an amiable chaꞏracter, and the ſtrongeſt proof of a ſound underſtanding.

The late King of Pruſſia, whom, when you have read his poſthumous volumes, you will conſider as a man of ſuperlative abiliꞏties, concludes his deſcription of every batꞏtle which he fought, with an impartial reꞏcapitulation of his own miſtakes, and freꞏquently with a generous acknowledgment of the better conduct of his enemy.

Beſides the vanity, in young men, of apꞏpearing to know more than any young man can poſſibly know, there is another ſpecies of pride to which youth in general is exꞏtremely prone. I mean that of appearing rich. Now, though no young man be weak enough to maintain, that riches imply the leaſt degree of merit in the poſſeſſor, yet the idle vanity of being ſuppoſed to have a large allowance to ſpend, is more generally the cauſe of ruin to ſtudents at the Univerꞏſity, than any natural propenſity to extraꞏvagance.

Every attempt to appear more learned, more knowing, more powerful, or richer than we really are, is fooliſh in the extreme; for, if we ſucceed at all in the deception, it

is

is of very fhort duration. In difpite of every effort to keep up the ball, it will foon come down, and will defcend with greater force in proportion to its height. The individual charaɛters of men, howfoever artfully fuftained, will infallibly vibrate to their true level in the opinion of the world, and the pretender will find himfelf at laft, like the fpirt of a fountain, even below the furface of his parent refervoir; below his natural level.

Vera gloria, fays the charming Cicero, *radices agit, atque etiam propagatur: fiɛta omnia celeriter, tanquam flofculi, decidunt, nec fimulatum poteft quidquam effe diuturnum.*

Vale.

LETTER V.

WE of the human species are diſtinguiſhed from what we call *the brute
creation*, not by the internal or external formation of our bodies; for, in theſe, the difference is found, by naturiliſts, too inſufficient to entitle us even to a ſeparate *Order* in the
claſs of Quadrupeds. The celebrated Linnæus has placed *Man* in the CLASS *Mamalia*,
which includes Quadrupeds and Whales; and
in the ORDER *Primates*, which, according
to his artificial ſyſtem, neceſſarily comprehends the genus *Veſpertilio*. He does not
even compliment us with a *generic* diſtinction. A *ſpecific* difference is all that we are
allowed: thus, *Homo rationalis*. I am ſorry
to obſerve, that even this *trivial* epithet is
more than we generally deſerve.

I am compelled to be thus ſevere on the
human *ſpecies* (for you obſerve we have no
pretenſion to a *generic* diſtinction) becauſe
mankind appears to me the leaſt rational
part of the creation: Therefore I would not
tranſlate the word rationalis *rational*; but,
capable of reaſoning.

Old

Old men are frequently cenfured for their want of indulgence to the natural follies of youth. Is it then neceffary that young men fhould be fools? If fo, what becomes of this fpecific epithet which alone divides them from the brute creation? Or, muft they rank with brutes until a certain age?

I am led to thefe animadverfions by obferving, that young men, on their firft ftarting into life, are generally governed fo abfolutely by that fool Fafhion, as totally to forget that they are rational creatures; and that in point of drefs (for of that only I am now fpeaking) they are ready to facrifice every idea of propriety, and even conveniency, to the ridiculous whim of any defpicable infect of what is called the *beau monde.*

You are not hence to conclude, that I would have a young gentleman too fcrupuloufly attentive to the rationality of his drefs. Something muft be facrificed to Fafhion; but a young man of found intellects will not, in compliance with the whim, even of a prince, run into extremes that are palpably abfurd. I would not have my fon a floven. Total negligence of drefs is an affront to fociety: it indicates either an ignorance or contempt of the world; but an

abfoabſolute Fop is a creature almoſt below contempt. Dreſs, in the eye of philoſophy, is an inconſiderable objeƈt; but it is an ob-jeƈt of no ſmall influence in the opinion of mankind. The opinion of the world is of great conſequence to a young man: on ſtrangers, propriety or impropriety of dreſs, make the firſt impreſſion. Firſt impreſſions are not eaſily obliterated; dreſs, therefore, howſoever inſignificant in the abſtraƈt, be-comes an objeƈt of importance to every member of ſociety, particularly to a young man on his firſt appearance in the great world.

You are become a member, and I hope you will prove not an unworthy member, of one of the firſt Univerſities in Europe; and of a college that has produced many eminent, very eminent men. But, alas! the number of men diſtinguiſhed for ſupe-rior knowledge and abilities, is far exceeded by the number of drones that have iſſued from the hive, and have mixed with the illi-terate part of mankind, undiſtinguiſhed and forgotten.

To what cauſe ſhall we attribute this la-mentable exceſs of ignorance, in the num-ber of perſons educated at Oxford and Cam-bridge?

bridge? It muſt, I think, be aſcribed to a variety of cauſes, partly acting upon each other, and ſome of them totally independent. The firſt cauſe, which operates alike in both Univerſities, is a poſitive adherence to ſtatutes and cuſtoms, which, not according with the preſent improved ſtate of learning, nor with the manners of the preſent times, fatigue and diſguſt the ſtudents immediately on their admiſſion. Extreme early riſing and conſtant attendance in the chapel, are hardſhips in which they perceive no utility. They comply with reluctance. They are diſguſted with an academical life. They reſide no longer than is abſolutely neceſſary, and they look forward with impatience to the day of their releaſe. In ſuch a temper, little improvement can be expected. No young man will apply to learning *con amore*, in a diſagreable ſituation.

I am, neverthelefs, far from thinking, that young gentlemen ſhould be entirely unreſtrained; but I am of opinion, that theſe reſtrictions ſhould be confined to their immoralities, and that in all other reſpects their reſidence at the Univerſity ſhould be rendered as agreeable to themſelves as poſſible. There is a principle in human nature fo averfe to coercion, particularly about the age of fixteen, that the lectures of your tutors make very little impreffion, becaufe they are attended by compulfion. In every other Univerfity in Europe, attendance upon lectures is a voluntary act: no tafks, no exercifes are impofed. Neverthelefs, the public lectures are univerfally attended, and the ftudents liften with an eager defire of information: becaufe their attendance is voluntary.

It cannot be denied, that the colleges in our Englifh Univerfities retain an obvious fimilitude to Roman Catholick Convents; and it is very furprizing that the Reformation fhould have produced fo little, fo very little, alteration in their inftitutes, habits and regulations; many of which are totally indefenfible on principles either of policy or utility.

In thefe ftrictures, I have told you nothing that you did not know before; nothing with which the whole world is not as well acquainted as myfelf: nor have I difcovered any blemifhes that are not feen and felt by every rational member of both Univerfities. Why then, you will afk, are no fteps taken towards reformation?

You

You remember Æfop's fable of the mice and the cat. Who will hang the bell? A firft Reformer is fure to create many enemies. It is very difficult to ftem and divert into another channel, a torrent of prejudice that has been fo many years accumulating, without being carried down with the ftream. But fuch a reformation requires a power which the Univerfities themfelves do not poffefs. It muft be the act of the Legiflature; and the Adminiftration, in this kingdom, is generally too deeply involved in national politicks, to fpare the time and application that a reform of fuch importance would require.

It is poffible that, in fome future period, a fortunate concurrence of circumftances may produce a rational and uniform fyftem of education in both Univerfities. There are now refident at Oxford and at Cambridge, men fully adequate to the delineation of a comprehenfive, an univerfal plan of academical tuition, which, with the advantages of their prefent foundations, might, very eafily, be rendered fuperior to any inftitutions of the kind in Europe. No other Univerfities poffefs fuch noble and fpacious edifices for the accommodation of ftudents;

no

no Univerſities are ſo munificently endow-
ed; no other Univerſities poſſeſs ſuch public and college libraries; and certainly no
ſeminaries of learning can boaſt ſo many
members of diſtinguiſhed erudition in every
branch of literature: but theſe ſingular advantages are ſacrificed to an unavoidable
(unavoidable, in the preſent ſtate of things)
compliance with ancient ſtatutes, manners,
and cuſtoms.

LET-

LETTER VI.

I HAVE, in my laſt letter, acknowledged the defects which foreigners obſerve in the general economy of Engliſh Univerſities. They are aſtoniſhed to find that our profeſſorſhips are commonly ſinecures; that there is no continued ſeries of public lectures in arts or ſciences; and that college tutors are almoſt the only ſources of information. This naturally creates ſurprize; becauſe, in all other Univerſities, the ſtudents have the advantage of daily public lectures, without vacation or interruption, during the greateſt part of every year. What is the cauſe of ſuch laborious attention of the profeſſors in theſe Univerſities?—The anſwer is obvious. They are paid by their auditors, who are under no obligation to attend them; conſequently their emoluments depend on their reputation.

Thus have I candidly, and without reſerve, recapitulated the articles of accuſation, which, in your hearing, have been frequently brought forward, in objection to an Engliſh academical education; and I will

now

now endeavour to anſwer theſe objections, ſo far as the ſubject may influence your purſuits.

Young men are naturally ſanguine in their expectations: they are impatient and diſſatisfied with every thing, which, according to their conceptions, falls ſhort of perfection. But a few years experience will infallibly convince them, that human inſtitutions are incapable of perfection, and that a prudent man will make the beſt uſe in his power of things as they are. That the preſent ſyſtem of education at Oxford and Cambridge might be improved, will be readily admitted; and, that a careful reviſion of the ſtatutes, and a conſequent abolition of many cuſtoms, ill adapted to the learning and manners of the preſent age, will take place, is more than probable. But, the fortuitous events neceſſary to bring forward ſo conſequential a revolution, depend on ſo ſingular a coalition of circumſtances, that many ages may yet roll on, before our Univerſities are perfectly reformed.

Let us now attend a little to facts. The arguments deduced from ſpeculation and theory are certainly againſt us. Our Uni-

                    verſities

verfities are governed by ancient ftatutes,
and habits apparently not calculated to produce, either learned men, or polite fcholars.
Yet thefe Univerfities have produced a Bacon, a Newton, a Locke, a Sanderfon, a
Bentley, a Tillotfon, a Sherlock, an Addifon, a Bolingbroke, a Steel, a Chefterfield,
a Pitt; befides many other learned men,
polite fcholars, and great ftatefmen. If therefore we may reafon from facts, an Englifh
Univerfity, with all its imperfections, is
fully competent to the communication of
claffical, philofophical, and polite literature
to their greateft extent: nor do we find that
any other feminaries, in this ifland or on
the continent, can exhibit a lift of worthies,
in any degree comparable with the gradu-
ates of Oxford and Cambridge, from the
latter end of the laft century to the prefent
time.

Yet this fact, indifputable as it may appear, does not prove the perfection of our
academical inftitutions; but it fufficiently
demonftrates the poffibility of acquiring at
Oxford or Cambridge, knowledge in a very
high degree, in every branch of literature;
and hence, we are fairly authorized to conclude,

clude, that the ignorance of thofe who difgrace the Univerfities, cannot with juftice
be afcribed to the want of opportunity.

To corroborate what I have faid in favour
of our Englifh Univerfities, and at the fame
time to relieve you, in fome degree, from the
didactic dulnefs of thefe parental epiftles, I
will endeavour to give you a fketch of the
portraits of fome of thofe men whom I have
mentioned as ornaments to the feminaries
in which they were educated.

Francis Bacon, the fon of Sir Nicholas
Bacon, Lord Keeper of the Great Seal, in
the reign of Elizabeth, was born in 1561.
In the twelfth year of his age, he was entered a Student of Trinity College, Cambridge. By this early admiffion, you perceive, that Students in the Univerfities,
during the firft three or four years, were
fchool boys; and hence, we may probably
account for the prevalent continuance of
grammatical and claffical learning, at one
Univerfity, and for the cuftom of fcholaftic
impofitions in both.

Such however was the genius and application of this boy, that, by the time he was
fixteen, he is faid to have completed the
circle of the fciences then taught, and to

                                  have

have been perfectly acquainted with the Ariftotelean philofophy; the abfurdity of which philofophy he immediately difcovered and finally refuted. What this philofophy was, I fhall tell you another time.

About the age of fixteen, an age when young gentlemen of the prefent times ufually enter the Univerfity, he quitted Cambridge, and was, foon after, fent by his father to Sir Amias Pawlet, who was then the Queen's ambaffador at the court of France. During his refidence at Paris, about the nineteenth year of his age, he wrote a fhort treatife *Of the State of Europe*. On the fudden death of his father, being deftitute of proper fupport, he returned to England and commenced ftudent of the Law, and with fuch fuccefs, that after paffing through the ufual gradations, he became Lord High Chancellor of England, and was created Vifcount St. Albans.

During this progrefs to the fummit of honour, power and emolument, he continued his philofophical ftudies with unremitting affiduity, and was doubtlefs, not only the firft Lawyer, but the *firft*, I might have faid, the *only* philofopher then in the world. But, alas!—I wifh, for the honour

of

of human nature, that I could draw a vail over the fequel of his ftory. This great, this very great man, wanted that integrity of character, that conftitutional virtue, without which, all other endowments are, to ufe the words of St. Paul, *founding brafs and tinkling cymbals.*—— He was accufed of having been influenced in his decrees by pecuniary bribes, received at various times, to a confiderable amount; and, though it appeared that his fervants were the only gainers by fuch malpractice, yet he pleaded guilty, and was fentenced to pay a fine of 40,000l. —— to be imprifoned during the King's pleafure, and to be for ever incapable of office.

These fevere pains and penalties were entirely remitted by the King (James I.) by whom, and by his favourite the Duke of Buckingham, the delinquent was now more than ever careffed. He had a penfion of 1200l. and an additional grant of 600l. from the Alienation office. His own eftate produced about 700l; fo that he retired to his philofophical ftudies with an income of 2,500l. per annum: neverthelefs, his debts, at the time of his death, amounted to 22,000l.

c 4

Thefe

Thefe facts, if facts they really be, feem ftrangely incongruous: yet they are well authenticated. It is moft probable that he was feduced by the King to plead guilty, in order to divert the ftorm of enquiry from falling on the head of Buckingham. If this be true, his character, deliniated by Pope, in the following lines, was moft juft.

" If parts allure thee, think how Bacon fhin'd,
The wifeft, brighteft, meaneft of mankind."

He feems to have been a fingular example of a mind capable of facrificing confcience, reputation and every rational fource of felicity, at the fhrine of Pluto, yet without avarice; and, what is more extraordinary, without being, in any degree, a fenfualift.

His moral character out of the queftion, he will always be remembered, as a principal ornament to the Univerfity in which he was educated, and as the prototype of the Newtonian philofophy. "He was, fays Mr. Walpole (in his *Catalogue of Noble Authors*) the Prophet of Arts *(Sciences*, he fhould have faid) which Newton was fent afterwards to reveal."

Probably the great Sir Ifaac would have found his way without a guide; neverthe-

lefs,

lefs, Bacon, doubtlefs, firft marked the path to true philofophy, which Newton afterwards purfued.

"Alas!"—exclaims Mr. Walpole—"that he who could command immortality, fhould have ftooped to the little ambition of power!"—This exclamation founds well: but there are readers, who, after a little analytical reflexion, might afk, whether a man of fuperior talents might not rationally prefer *the little ambition of power*, to the *great ambition of immortal fame?* a reality to a phantom. A man of Bacon's talents might have wifhed for power for the fake of his country. Probably a conftitutional indolence was the caufe of his inattention to the cuftomary venality of his dependents: yet perhaps not *indolence*, but a predominant propenfity to philofophical thinking. That in winking at the venality of his fervants, he did not act from principle, may, I think, be juftly inferred from the following paffage in his Effay on Judicature.

" For that which concerns Clerks, and Minifters: the place of Juftice is an hallowed place, and therefore not only the bench, but the foot-pace, and precincts, and pur-

prife

prife thereof, ought to be preferved without fcandal and corruption."

To find a man of Bacon's fuperior abilities act, whether from indifference or from attention to other objects, diametrically oppofite to his own principles, is rather a painful difcovery: fuch examples however are not without their utility. They teach us that the good faculties of the brain, without the good faculties of the heart, are totally infufficient to form an eftimable character. Confcious integrity of conduct, would have afforded Bacon more real felicity than all his wealth, his power and philofophical immortality.

I am, &c.

LETTER VII.

JOHN MILTON, the celebrated author of *Paradife Loft*, was born in London in the year 1608, imbibed the rudiments of his education at St. Paul's fchool, thence was admitted of Chrift College, Cambridge, where, at the age of 24, he took his fecond degree in Arts. His father intended him for the church; but he was now become an enthufiaft in the religion which was afterwards the inftrument of Cromwell's ufurpation. Mufic and poetry were his favourite ftudies. His *Comus, l'Allegro, il Penferofo*, and *Lycidas*, were written foon after he left the Univerfity. They are poems, with which, when you have leifure to read for amufement, you will be exceedingly delighted.

About the year 1638, Milton made the tour of France and Italy. During his refidence at Florence, he wrote fome Latin verfes, in confequence of which, Salvaggi of Rome fent him this diftich,

Græcia Meonidem jactat fibi Roma Maronem:
Anglia Miltonum jactat utrique parem.

Mr.

Mr. Dryden, many years after, took the hint, and wrote the following lines in praise of Milton,

Three poets in three diftant ages born,
Greece, Italy and England did adorn:
The firft in majefty of thought furpafs'd,
The next in gracefulnefs, in both the laft.
The force of Nature could no farther go,
To make a third fhe join'd the former two.

At Naples, he became acquainted with the celebrated Baptifta Manfo, who at his departure complimented him thus,

Ut mens, forma, décor, facies, mos, fi pietas fic,
Non Anglus, verum, Hercule! angelus ipfe fores.

To underftand the meaning of this *fi pietas fic*, you muft know, that Milton was fo imprudent a bigot, as to avow his Prefbyterian opinions in the midft of bigots to an oppofite creed.

On his return to England in 1639, he commenced mafter of an academy in Alderfgate ftreet, in which occupation he continued till the execution of Charles I. and the confequent ufurpation of Oliver Cromwell, by whom he was appointed Latin Secretary to the Counfel of State. In 1652

he

he became blind, neverthelefs, he continued in his office till the reftoration of Charles II. who, notwithftanding Milton's virulent writings in oppofition to that reftoration, included him in the general amnefty. He now retired to a fmall houfe in the Artillery-walk, leading to Bunhill-fields, where he finifhed his Paradife Loft. He died in 1674, aged 66.

Paradife Loft, the *opus majus* of this our only heroic poet — except Glover, whofe Leonidas poffeffes confiderable merit — you will read with great delight; particularly as it will frequently bring to your memory many fublime paffages in Homer and Virgil. Doublefs it has fome blemifhes, which a reader of chafte difcernment and claffical tafte, will eafily perceive; but thefe blemifhes are abundantly counterpoized by a fublimity of imagination and harmony of numbers, equal, if not fuperior, to the moft admired poems of antiquity. If you fhould ever wifh to read Italian poetry — this idea obtrudes itfelf rather abruptly — no matter: if I had now fuffered it to efcape, it might poffibly never have recurred — If, I fay, you fhould ever wifh to be acquainted with the Italian poets — and fome of them

deferve

deferve your acquaintance — let me advife you to read Rolli's Tranflation of *Paradife Loft*, with the original before you. Thofe who are fuperficially acquainted with the Italian language, will fuppofe it incapable of reflecting Milton's fublimity; but they will find themfelves miftaken. The Italian language, though foft and fluent, is neverthelefs copious and comprehenfive. Rolli, in his tranflation, has loft very few of Milton's ideas.

He was buried in St. Giles' church, Cripple-gate. In 1737 a monument of Milton was erected in Weftminfter Abbey, at the expence of Mr. William Benfon, auditor of the impreft. If you wifh to know more of Milton, you will find various Lives of him in the Libraries, particularly thofe by Toland, Philips, Richardfon, Fenton, Birch; and in the *Biographia Britannica*, you will fee the facts in thefe feveral Lives concentered.

I fhall now give you a fketch of a man whom all nations acknowledged to have been the glory of human nature: the man of whom our moft correct and moft harmonious poet, hath faid with great felicity of imagination,

"Superior

" Superior Beings when of late they faw
A mortal man unfold all Nature's law,
Admir'd fuch wifdom in an earthly fhape
And fhew'd a Newton as we fhew an Ape."

Thefe lines, probably, are not new to you; but there is fo much originality in the idea, that it is almoft impoffible to think of NEWTON without repeating them.

He was born on Chriftmas-day, 1642, at Woolftrop in Lincolnfhire; received the early part of his education in the grammar-fchool at Grantham, and was admitted, at the age of eighteen, of Trinity College, Cambridge. At this time mathematics were pretty generally taught by the Tutors. The firft book put into young Newton's hand, was *Euclid's Elements*. He caft his eye over it, and was immediately mafter of every propofition. He thought the book too eafy to deferve much attention; but he after-wards acknowledged his miftake, and was forry for it. In 1665, that is, in his 22d year, he invented the *method of Fluxions*, by the help of which, he is faid, in the fpace of two years, to have carried the doctrine of *infinite feries* almoft to perfection. You will know what this means, when you become acquainted with the writings of this human prodigy.

prodigy. In 1667 he was elected Fellow of his College; in the same year he took his Master of Arts degree, and two years after, on the resignation of Dr. Barrow, was chosen Professor of Mathematics. During the first three years after his elevation to this dignity, he read lectures on Optics, and on communicating his theory of light and colours to the Royal Society, he was, in 1672, elected F.R.S.

This new theory of Light and Colours, though perfectly true, met with considerable opposition, and prevented him from publishing his Lectures on Optics. His subsequent discovery of that universal principle in Nature, called *gravity*, by which he explained, in the most satisfactory manner, the vast system of the universe, shared, for a time, the same fate. Men were unwilling, at once, to relinquish the then established philosophy of Des Cartes, with whose theory of the universe, the world in general was satisfied.

This French philosopher, Des Cartes, was a man of considerable abilities, an able geometrician, and of an inventive genius. At the time of his appearance in France, the philosophy of Aristotle was taught in

all

all Univerfities in Europe. This prevalent philofophy, he, in a great meafure, overturned. He began by proving the exiftence of *matter* in oppofition to Ariftotle, who faid, *non eft quid, nec quantum nec quale.*

I will now give you a fketch of the hypothetical fyftem of this celebrated French philofopher. — He imagined three diftinct fpecies of elements.

1ft. Infinitely minute, and of no determined figure, but confifting of particles ready to adapt themfelves to every interftice between the globules which compofe the fecond, and thereby prevent a vacuum.

2dly. An element compofed of atoms perfectly fpherical, produced by the continued friction of the angular and more grofs particles of the third element, which being firft created and fuppofed to be rapidly whirled round its centre — *circa centra fua gyrare* — gradually rubbed off its angles, and thefe filings — *ramenta illa quæ e corporibus eruuntur* — formed the firft element that filled up the chinks.

3dly. An element compofed of the grofs particles of matter, exceeding the firft and fecond in magnitude, lefs fit for motion,

D

but

but better calculated for adhesion. These form the grosser bodies.

Sol et *Fixæ* are composed of the first element; *Cælum* of the first and second; opake bodies, such as comets and planets, of the third.

According to this philosopher, rarefaction is caused by the introduction of celestial matter into the pores of denser bodies: *causa ordinaria*, he says, *ignis est, quia cum particulæ materiæ subtilis, quibus constat, in continuo sint motu, facile aliorum corporum meatus ingrediuntur atque illos dilatant et extendunt.*

Gravitation he explains thus: Dense bodies having less propensity to fly from the centre round which they are whirled, remain nearest that centre, where they are constantly pressed by the more subtile elements. In answer to the objection, that, according to this hypothesis, bodies falling to the Earth should descend with most rapidity at first, passing then through the thinest medium, he says — *Diversitatem lapidis inde oriri, quod lapidis, in suo descensu, motus precedentis et insuper augmentum recepit, ab impulsu materiæ subtilis.*

In speaking of compound motion, he says,
— *Omnia*

—Omnia enim motus qui a duabus aut pluribus caufis pendet, eft compofitus: fo a ball out of a canon defcribes a curve towards the Earth, becaufe its direct progrefs is impeded by the air, and becaufe heavy bodies defcend floweft at firft.

Such were the philofophical opinions of the celebrated Des Cartes: opinions which, as they were built on *the bafelefs fabric of a vifion*, would in time have *melted into thin air*; but the fudden oriental blaze of our great philofophical luminary, difpelled them like a morning mift before the fun. The fimple power of gravitation appeared at firft an hypothefis; but it was an hypothefis confirmed by experiment, and demonftratively explanatory of the motions of the planets that conftitute our folar fyftem. This fyftem, and the Newtonian philofophy in general, 1 may probably delineate more at large in fome future letters. I fhall finifh the prefent biographically.

Mr. Newton's celebrated *Philofophiæ Naturalis Principia Mathematica*, was firft publifhed in 1687, by the Royal Society, under the infpection of Dr. Halley. In the following year, he was elected member of Parliament for the Univerfity of Cambridge;

in

in 1696, was made Warden, and three years after, Mafter of the Mint, a place worth 1500l. per annum. In 1703, he was chofen Prefident of the Royal Society, which he continued during the remainder of his life. He died in the year 1727, aged 85, and was buried in Weftminfter Abbey, where you will find his tomb on the left hand, at the entrance into the choir; which tomb, I dare fay, you will vifit with more heart-felt veneration than Mahomedans feel at the fhrine of their prophet at Mecca, or Roman Catholicks at Loretto.

I forgot to tell you, that he was knighted by Queen Ann, in the year 1705. It was a trivial circumftance, fcarce worth notice in the life of a Newton, on whom titles conferred by princes, could perpetuate no honour, except to themfelves.

JOHN LOCKE, univerfally remembered, as the author of the *Effay on Human Under-ftanding*, was born at Wrington in Somer-fetfhire, in 1632. He was firft educated at Weftminfter fchool, and thence became a Student of Chrift-church, Oxford, where he took his degrees in Arts. In 1664, he went abroad as Secretary to Sir William Swan,

Envoy

Envoy to the Elector of Brandenburgh. In the following year he returned to Oxford, and was soon after introduced to Lord Afhley (afterwards Earl of Shaftfbury) who being made Chancellor, appointed him Secretary of Prefentations. The plan of his celebrated *Effay* was fketched in 1670. In 1675, Mr. Locke took the degree of Bachelor of Phyfic, and the fame year went to Montpelier for the recover of his health, where he continued till the year 1679. In 1682, his patron fled to Holland, to illude a profecution for high treafon, where he foon died. Mr. Locke attended him in his exile, and did not return to England till 1688, the year of the revolution. On his arrival in England, he retired to the feat of Sir Francis Marfham, where he fpent moft of his time. In 1695, King William appointed him a Commiffioner of Trade and Plantations, which office he refigned in 1700, and died in 1704, aged 73.

Mr. Locke was, doubtlefs, a man of very ftrong intellects; very capable of intenfe thinking, and peculiarly happy in the arrangement of his ideas. His *Effay on Human Underflanding* is Logick divefted of its ancient technical formality. It is a book

that

that you will read with great pleasure and profit, as soon as you are capable of close application. Intense thinking is an operation of the mind, to which, at school, you were not accustomed. It is a habit of which young minds are incapable, and, like strength of body, to be acquired only by gradual exercise. But, though Locke be very justly considered as a classical author at the Universities, let me advise you never implicitly to submit your own reason to any of his opinions. Whenever you are not perfectly convinced, mark the passage, and dispute the matter with your companions. Remember however in all your disputations, that the discovery of truth is your sole object; that it is of no consequence whether it be found by your antagonist or yourself; that an honest disputant will admit the arguments of his opponent in all their energy; that every species of sophism is inadmissible; and that the least appearance of passion is not only disadvantageous to the disputant, but is, at the same time, a decided proof of his want of that urbanity, which distinguishes a gentleman from those who have not had the advantage of a liberal education.

I have dwelt a little upon this subject of

dis-

difputation, becaufe pertinacity is a common, I had almoft faid an univerfal vice of
young men. I well remember it in myfelf.
I well remember that I was moft tenacious,
of my opinions, when I was moft ignorant;
and that, in proportion as I acquired more
knowledge, I became more diffident. Since
I kneel at the chair of confeffion, I will
tell you, very honeftly, that I recollect many
inftances in myfelf, of juvenile arrogance
and felf-fufficiency, for which I ought to
have been feverely chaftized. My father had
from Nature too much of *the milk of human
kindnefs* to treat me as I deferved.

Here I clofe my biographical fketches for
the prefent. Bacon, Milton, Newton, Locke,
are the four great pillars which fupport the
monument of Britifh genius: a monument,
which, without national partiality, we may
affirm, ftands eminently fuperior to that of
any other nation. I have fpoken of them
chronologically; but, Sir Ifaac Newton,
doubtlefs, deferves the firft place in the
group. Bacon had the merit of difcovering, that former philofophers began at the
wrong end; that philofophical doctrines
built upon hypothetical principles, were incapable of demonftration, and therefore

 might

might be falfe; and that all found philofophy muft be founded on facts proved by
experiment. This Bacon faw; but he went
no farther. Like Mofes, from Pifgah, he
beheld the land of promife at a diftance;
but Newton led the hoft into the Canaan
of Philofophy.

I am, &c.

LETTER VIII.

OBSERVING the various fortunes of young men, issuing from the same school, with the same advantages, and apparently of equal capacity, some philosophers have been induced to ascribe the exaltation or depression of individuals, to a power which they call an irresistible destiny. The consequence of this Calvinistical tenet is absurd, because it is incompatible with every principle of morality: the difficulty of a logical proof of this absurdity, arises from the impossibility of tracing effects to their causes.

You are probably not unacquainted with the amusement on a bowling-green. Every competitor aims his bowl at the *jack*, and the course of his bowl is determined partly by the constitutional bias of the bowl, and partly by the direction communicated in the moment of bowling. This constitutional bias is given to the bowl by a certain quantity of lead, and its indirect, curvilineal propensity is greater, and consequently more difficult to counteract, in proportion to the

quantity

quantity of metal in its compofition. But a bias may be given by other metals: gold is yet heavier than lead, and a natural levity in the wood, will give equal effect to a lefs quantity of either. A ftudent may be biafed by too much lead, by too much gold, or negatively biafed by too much levity. But, to continue the fimile, are we therefore to conclude, that a fkilful bowler has it not in his power to give his bowl the true direction to the goal. Would not fuch an artift laugh at the Predeftinarian who fhould endeavour to convince him that he was not, in this inftance, a free agent, and that his fuccefs did not depend entirely on his free will and dexterity.

Hence, I think, we may rationally conclude, that every effect is the natural confequence of a fufficient caufe, and, to fpeak in the language of mathematicians, that the fortunes of men are *generally* in a direct ratio of their prudence and abilities.

Without abilities to a certain degree, and alfo without a certain quantum of fchool learning, it is impoffible for a young man to cut any figure at the Univerfity; but the moft diftinguifhed abilities, with all the claffical learning that a fchoolboy can poffi-

bly

bly acquire, are not of themfelves fufficient
to lift a young gentleman to that degree of
notice, to which, a truly liberal mind will
naturally afpire. His parts, his learning,
without prudence are of little value. Like
a fhip without balaft, he becomes the fport
of every wind, and is in perpetual danger
of deftruction.

Remember what I am now going to fay.
I mean to fpeak very emphatically, becaufe
it is the hinge on which your future fortunes will turn. I mean *your choice of companions*. It is a matter of infinite importance. Young men, on their firft arrival at
the Univerfity, naturally look up to thofe
who have been fome time matriculated; they
liften to their information with compla-
cency, and too implicitly imbibe their opinions of men and things. "Such a Profeffor
is a ftupid fellow — fuch a tutor is a tedious
blockhead — fuch a duty is a *bore*." This is
a language which you will frequently hear.
But you will very foon difcover, that thefe
orators are generally indolent, illiterate,
weak young men; totally infenfible to that
thirft of knowledge, that noble enthufiafm,
that glorious ambition with which the great
luminaries of fcience were infpired, and without

out which, all expectations of pre-eminence are vain.

Morofenefs in a young man is unamiable and unnatural; but there is a certain degree of referve neceffary on his firft admiffion into a numerous fociety. Intimate connexions are more eafily avoided than broken. I do not wifh by this caution to taint your mind with fufpicion; but remember, that *evil communications corrupt good manners,* and that in friendfhip with a vicious character, you are conftantly walking on the brink of a precipice. How confident foever you may be of your own fafety, the moment he flips, he will certainly lay hold of your gown, and down you tumble headlong together.

I am very forry to hear that in the Univerfities

Sunt qui nec veteris pocula Maffici
Nec partem folido demere de die
Spernunt.

Fortunately, in this kingdom, drinking is rather an expenfive vice, and therefore neceffarily confined to a part of the community. It cannot much interrupt the ftudies of thofe, who come to the Univerfity, merely

with

with an intention of whiling away a few years which they knew not how otherwife to employ. But thefe young noblemen and gentlemen, will foon be too fatally convinced, that early drinking will infallibly deftroy their conftitutions, impair their intellects, and fhorten their lives. I fpeak as a phyfician: if there be a power on Earth, whofe intereft it is, gradually to annihilate the ftrength and political importance of this nation, no means could be devifed half fo effectual, as that of alluring the fons of noblemen and gentlemen of rank and fortune, to premature debauchery.

You are not hence to conclude, that Nature gradually ripens men for vice. Vice is at all times, and in every ftage of our exiftence, a moft induftrious enemy to health, and confequently to life; but at any age, before the body has attained its *acme*, every fpecies of debauchery is doubly deftructive: and, were it even poffible that an herculean conftitution fhould, in time, recover the effect of juvenile imprudence, the refolution neceffary to conquer vicious habits is fo rarely found, that early debauchery generally ends in premature imbecility, and decrepitude both of body and mind.

But

But the vice of *drinking to excefs*, muft not be imputed exclufively to the Univerfities. Its fource lies frequently fomewhat higher. I am forry to fay, that this infidious enemy to human nature, often originates in our public fchools. Shame to tell! the prefent age affords many examples of drunken fchoolboys. What can be the caufe of an evil fo enormous? Who are we to cenfure? —The mafters?—No. They do every thing in their power to prevent it; but in vain. It originates in the inconceivable folly of opulent parents, who, by fending their darling fons, after every vacation, with guineas in their pockets, furnifh them with the temptations to every kind of irregularity. Not only drunkennefs is the confequence of this oftentatious parental weaknefs, but other vices that are often feverely felt in the third and fourth generation. ·

Many young gentlemen fail down the tide of indulgence for want of capacity, or reflexion, to perceive the rocks and quickfands, amongft which their voyage muft terminate. Thefe deferve our compaffion. But, what fhall we fay of thofe, on whom nature has beftowed penetration and forefight, amply fufficient to know the confe-

quences

quences of vice and folly? Such young men are impelled by the pride of wealth, which enables them to be irregular; or by the pride of daring to be vicious; or by example; or by evil habits contracted at Eton or Weſt-minſter. Both theſe are noble inſtitutions; they are upon the whole well regulated; but the beſt regulations and the moſt ſevere attention of the maſters, will never prevent juvenile debauchery, ſo long as parents are ſo fooliſh as to furniſh their children with the means.

We expect you to dinner to morrow. By obſerving the following directions, you may avoid the extreme dirt of our village.

TO Trumpington tramping to viſit the Doctor,
Which ſure you may do without dread of a Proctor,
The village when juſt you begin to approach;
Before you arrive at the *Horſes and Coach*,
Lo! a path on your right — to gain which, with-
  out fail
Clap your hand on the poſt and ſkip over the rail.
Then follow your noſe 'till you come to the church,
And thus you will leave all the mud in the lurch.
You now muſt proceed to the ſouth of that ſteeple
Whoſe five brazen tongues call, in vain, the deaf
  people.

Behold,

Behold, on your left, a white gate — once fublime!
But all human grandeur muft yield to old Time.
That gate thro' which Anftey, when feiz'd with
    devotion,
Forth iffued — tho' that was not oft, I've a notion.
Perhaps for the chirping of birds he'd no relifh:
'Tis not heavenly mufic, 'tis true — rather hellifh.
I muft tell the truth, if I forfeit my neck for't,
The fparrows are often much louder than Heck-
    ford.
If I were the parfon, for fake of the fun,
I'd fhoot all thefe birds, if I borrow'd a gun.
Perhaps that might clafh with the Canons, or Ru-
    brick,
Or of glafs it might coft fome new pains, or a new
    brick.
No matter; the parifh muft pay, to a farthing,
Repairs of the Church, in Accounts of Church-
    warding.
    Now enter the gate, and now put off your fhoes,
For 'tis all holy ground, 't was the feat of that Mufe,
That whilom the Trumpington Bard did infpire:
Here he fung the *Bath Guide* — Here fhe tun'd his
    fweet lyre:
That poem delightful to youth and to fages
Of this prefent age, and of all future ages.
Alas! of that Bard's rich poetical treafure,
Here nothing remains, but of verfe the fame mea-
    fure.

So

So coiners of brafs, of the die in poffeffion,
To fixpences give but external impreffion.
No matter: tho' this may not prove current coin,
You'll find on the table an honeft Sir Loin.
The time you remember, for Time's on the wing:
We wait not a moment paft *three*, for the King.

Adieu!

E

LETTER IX.

YOU will hardly find yourself settled in your cell, before you will be informed by some of your fellow Students, that you are to read Logick; a Science of which you cannot have formed any idea. It is derived from Λoγoς, *sermo, verbum,* and was at first considered as the art of-conversing or rather disputing. Zeno, a Greek philosopher, who lived about 450 years before Christ, is said to have been the inventor of this art, if an art it may be called. It was afterwards particularly cultivated by the Greek sect of of philosophers, called the *Peripatetics,* of whom Aristotle was the chief.

When you are better acquainted with the history of literature, you will learn, that, after the destruction of the Roman empire, many ages elapsed before the revival of any art or science. You will also learn, that, after this revival, the writings of Aristotle became the Gospel of Philosophy, and that his books were classical in every part of Europe till the beginning of the last century. About that time *Des Cartes,* published a

new

new fyftem of Philofophy, different, but not lefs chimerical, than that of Ariftotle. It prevailed, however, particularly in France, until our immortal Newton publifhed his *Principia*; which, being founded on facts, neceffarily refuted all former hypothetical opinions.

The philofophy of Ariftotle, and of *Des Cartes*, is now totally difregarded and forgotten: yet the Logick of the prefent day is fundamentally that of Ariftotle, whofe fyftem *Des Cartes* new-modelled and corrected. He divided his book into four parts, viz. *De mentis perceptione—De judicio feu propofitione—De ratiocinatione feu fyllogifmo—De methodo feu difpofitione.* This divifion has been generally adopted by fubfequent writers on this fubject. Le Clerc, however, one of the beft of them, entitles his four divifions, *De ideis—De judiciis—De methodo—De argumentatione.*

Ariftotle, and his difciples, divided the objects of thought or *entia*, into ten claffes, *categoria*, or *prædicamenta*; all which, except the firft, they called Accidents. Thefe are they: *Subftantia, Quantitatis, Qualitatis, Relationis, Actionis, Paffionis, Ubi, Quand, Situs, Habitus.*

On

On thefe principles, the Ariftotelian Lo-gicians difputed with great fubtilty, and to very little purpofe, in every Univerfity in Europe, till about the year 1630, when Des Cartes publifhed his Philofophy, which, in a little time, rofe into reputation on the ruins of Ariftotle.

A great variety of books on Logick, tran-flated or tranfcribed from Ariftotle and Des Cartes, were written and publifhed in the laft century. Of the prefent century I re-collect no book of any note on this fubject, except *Watts* and *Duncan*, both in our own language. The laft of thefe, I underftand, is the book now generally recommended by the Tutors at Cambridge, to be read by ftu-dents of the firft year. It has fome merit in point of arrangement; but it wants per-fpicuity; it contains many unneceffary re-petitions, and is frequently inaccurate even in point of grammar. Why this art, which in our Univerfities is never publickly exer-cifed but in Latin, fhould be ftudied in Englifh, I cannot underftand. Perhaps you will afk, to what purpofe is it ftudied at all?

We muft not be too ready with our *cui bono?* The Logick of the *Peripatetics*, I confefs, is little better than a ufelefs jargon;

and

and even the beſt ſyſtem of Logick, conſidered only as the art or inſtrument of diſputation, is more likely to confound truth than diſcover it. A public logical diſputation reſembles much the practice, in former times, of ſeeking truth by ſingle combat. He that was moſt dexterous in the uſe of his weapons, whether a true or a falſe Knight, always proved victorious. Logick, I think, might as well have marched into oblivion with Knight-errantry, Juſts and Tournaments. Neverthelefs, if I diveſt Logick of its Ariſtotelian jargon; if I call it the art of *thinking*, not of *wrangling*; or rather, if I call it not an *art* but a *ſcience*, the knowledge of myſelf, of the origin and progreſs of my own ideas; a ſyſtem of Logick will then appear a delineation, a chart of the human underſtanding, and conſequently an object highly deſerving my attention.

But ſuppoſe it to be of no uſe as an inſtrument of inveſtigation, it is univerſally conſidered as a branch of Academical learning; no young gentleman therefore would run the rifk of appearing ignorant of Logick as an art, its terms, and conſtruction. Beſides, as the Univerſities chuſe to make it

the

the ladder to honours, it would be foolifh to kick it down till you have done with it.

The following Outline of this Art of Reafoning will give you a general idea of the fubject; without which, you would read your *Duncan* the firft time over, almoft entirely in the dark. I have thrown the whole into four tables; which, being compared with the book as you proceed, will confiderably affift your memory.

TABLE

TABLE I. LOGICK.

Logick

Perception
- Ideas, whence
- Ideas simple
- Ideas of substances
- Ideas of the mind
  - Ideas compound
  - Ideas abstract
  - Ideas of relations
- Ideas, words the signs of
- Definition
- Composition and resolution

Judgment
- Judgment, grounds of
- Propositions, affirmat. and negat.
- Prop. particular and universal
- Prop. absolute and conditional
- Prop. simple and compound
- Prop. selfevident and demonstrat.

Reasoning
- In general, and its parts
- Its object; to determine gen. & species
- Regarding powers and properties
- Forms of Syllogisms
- Demonstration

Method
- In general
  - Analytic, tracing things backward to their source.
  - Synthetic, deducing things from their first principles.
- Of Science, is that certain knowledge which we derive from the contemplation of our own Ideas, deduced from intuitive propositions.

TABLE

Table II. PERCEPTION.

Ideas, original from
{
Senfation, as of Light, Darkneſs, Heat, Cold, &c.
or Reflexion, as of Thinking, Doubting, Believing.
}

Ideas, ſimple from
{
Senfation, as Qualities, viz. Sound, Colour, Smell.
or Reflexion, as Perception, Volition, &c.
or from both: as Ideas of Pleaſure, Pain, Power, Unity.
}

Ideas of Subſtances.
{
Material. The union of Properties or Qualities, viz. Gold, Water, Man. Qualities or Modes are Eſſential or Accidental.
or Immaterial, called Spirit.
}

Ideas, framed by the Mind.
{
Compound, when many ſimple Ideas are united, as in Beauty, Gratitude, Harmony, an Inch, a Mile, a Square, a Circle.
Abſtract: i. e. when ſeparated from the circumſtances that render the Idea particular: it becomes general, viz. à □, a O, &c.
Relative, or Comparative, as Greater, Leſs, Older, Father, Son, &c.
}

Ideas, words the ſigns of. But ſimple Ideas not being definable — as, White, Red — words are capable of communicating complex Ideas only, unleſs the ſimple Ideas exiſted already in the mind of the perſon with whom we converſe; but complex Ideas may be defined, as *Animal, Rational, &c.*

Definition: explains the meaning of words that ſtand for complex Ideas. — Definition of the Names of things is arbitrary and admits of no diſpute: but, of the thing, is capable of proof and may therefore be doubted. Definitions are deſcriptions of Ideas in the mind.

Compoſition and Reſolution of our Ideas. In definitions we ſhould begin with Claſs, thence deſcend to Orders, thence to Genera, thence to Species, thence to Individuals.

TABLE

TABLE III. JUDGMENT.

Judgment from
- Intuition: the immediate perception of the agreement or difagreement of any two Ideas: *The whole is greater than any of its parts.* The foundation of Scientific Knowledge.
- Experience: the foundation of Natural Knowledge.
- Teftimony: the foundation of Hiftory.

Propofitions are Judgments put into words, affirming two or more Ideas to agree or difagree. They confift of
- Subject = *God*
- Copula = *is*
- Predicate = *omnipotent.*

If a negative particle be added to the Copula, the Subject and Predicate are difjoined: it is then called a negative Pred.

Propofitions
- Univerfal; the figns of which are *all, every, none, no. All men are mortal.* Here the Predicate applies to every individual of the Subject.
- Particular; the figns of which are *some, a few, a part. Some Students are blockheads.* Here fortunately the Predicate applies but to part of the Subject.

Propofitions
- Abfolute: *God is infinitely wife.*
- Conditional: *If a Stone be expofed to the Sun, it will contract heat.* Here the Predicate is not neceffarily connected with the Subject.

Propofitions
- Simple, have one Subject and one Predicate: *God is juft.*
- Compound
  - have 2 Subjects and 1 Predicate: *God is wife and powerful*——or 1 Subject and 2 Predicates: *Kings are neither exempt from Pain nor Death*——or 2 Subjects and 2 Predicates: *Riches and Honours elate the Mind and increafe our Defires.*

Propofitions
- Selfevident: *It is impoffible for the fame thing to be and not to be.* Speculative Propofitions are Mathematical *Axioms;* Practical Propofitions are *Poftulata.*
- Demonftrative: *The World had a biginning.* Speculative, 47th of the 1ft book of Euclid. Practical, to defcribe a fquare on a given right line.

Table IV. REASONING.

Reasoning in general is an operation of the mind deducing some unknown Propositions, from others that are known. These previous Propositions, which are called the *Major* and *Minor* of a Syllogism, are, in a simple act of Reasoning, two in number, and must be intuitive truths.
Major: *Every creature possessed of reason and liberty is accountable for his actions.*
Minor: *Man is a creature possessed of reason and liberty.*

Reasoning, its object. To rank things under universal Ideas, called *genera*; and to separate these into *species*.
Killing is the genus of which *Murder* and *Manslaughter* are species.

Reasoning, regarding powers and properties of things, and the relations of our general Ideas. The object of reasoning is to discover and ascribe to things their attributes and properties, by a skilful application of intermediate Ideas. To do this requires some general knowledge and particularly mathematical knowledge.

Syllogisms, have 4 figures
1. Middle term Subject of the Major and Predicate of the Minor.
2. Middle term the Predicate of both.
3. Middle term the Subject of both.
4. Middle term Predicate of Major and Subject of the Minor.

Moods of Syllogisms
Quantity { Universal / Particular
Quality { Affirmative / Negative.

Syllogisms hypothetical or conditional: the Major always consists of Antecedent and Consequent, the first implying the latter.
Modus ponens, admits the Antecedent in the Minor.
Modus tollens: the Minor rejects the Consequent.
Enthymemes: when one of the Propositions is not-expressed.

Table

TABLE IV. continued.

Reasoning by {

Series, in which the Predicate of one simple Syllogism becomes the Subject of the next, and so on, till the Subject of the first, and Predicate of the last unite in the conclusion.

Induction affirms of the whole what is true of all its parts: thus — *Quadrupeds move, Birds move, Fishes move, Insects move, ergo all Animals move.*

Dilemma proves the absurdity of an assertion. If the Major be affirmative, the conclusion will be negative, and vice versa: so Euclid proves two figures to be equal, by shewing the absurdity of supposing them greater or less.

Demonstration is a Series of Syllogisms whose premises are either definitions, selfevident truths, or propositions already established. Demonstration is *Direct* or *Indirect*.

LET-

LETTER X.

THAT during your refidence at the Charter Houfe, you have forgotten all you knew of Arithmetic before your admition, is no great wonder; nor is it any great misfortune. Arithmetic, (derived, you know, from αριθμὸς and μέτρον) is a Science which fchool boys learn only as a mechanical art: they are taught, by certain rules, to pile up numbers and pull them down again, as, by way of amufement, they would the *men* of a Backgammon-table, without the leaft comprehenfion of the reafon for the rule, the powers of the numbers with which they work, or the nature of the operation. But when Arithmetic is firft propofed, as a new Science, to a young man capable of reflexion, he contemplates its appearance with the fame inquifitive eye, the fame curiofity, the fame defire of information, that he would behold a ftranger poffeffing powers that could reach to the very gates of infinity.

Such a Student will probably reafon thus. " Here are ten fymbolical characters, 1, 2, 3, 4, 5, 6, 7, 8, 9, 0; with which, when I

am

am acquainted with their ufe, I fhall not only fignify diftinctly the greateft imaginable numbers; but fhall alfo be able by an artful pofition and dexterous ufe of them, to anfwer the moft difficult queftions in which numbers are concerned. The enlightened Greeks and Romans knew nothing of thefe ten magical figures: they were, it feems, invented by the Arabians. It appears to have been an invention infinitely ingenious and important, and I now ardently wifh for a philofophical acquaintance with thefe inftruments."

The firft fingularity which you will obferve in thefe Arabian figures, is that, when any number of them fucceed each other, we eftimate them, as we read the Hebrew language, from right to left, thus, 796. The firft figure on the right hand is *fix units*; the fecond, *nine tens*; the third, *feven hundreds*. If to thefe three figures I add three more, thus 428,796, they alfo exprefs, like the firft three, units, tens, hundreds; the 8 is eight thoufand units, the 2 is twice ten thoufand or twenty thoufand units, and the 4 is four hundred thoufand units. If to thefe I add a feventh figure, it will exprefs fo many millions of units, an eighth figure

fo many tens of millions of units, and fo
on: thus you perceive all numeration, be
the fum ever fo great, is no more than a
repetition of the denominations of the three
firft figures.

Thefe obfervations may appear trivial.
Euclid's Geometry is built on felf-evident
propofitions, which, to a learner, always feem
trifling. It is impoffible to begin the ftudy
of any Science too near its fource.

We now proceed to the firft and moft
fimple operation of Arithmetic called *Addition:* for example

    To 25, the quarter of a hundred
    Add 75, three quarters of a hundred
    ———
Sum 100

I reafon thus, 5 and 5 make 10; but I
cannot put down ten in the unite's place,
therefore I carry in my mind, this ten to
the 7, which ftands in the ten's place; thus
the 7 becomes an 8, and this 8 added to the
2, makes ten tens. Now ten tens make one
hundred; therefore I write a cypher in the
ten's place and a *one* in that of hundreds:
for, as I have but ten figures to work with,
and as each of thefe expreffes units only, I
can put down, after each addition, no more

than the number of units less than ten.
The number of tens evidently belongs to the
next column on the left hand; for, suppose
I am adding the second column from the
right, though I do nothing more than add
units together, yet, occupying the second
place, they are tens. In like manner, every
ten in the third column is ten hundred, and
must therefore be carried to the fourth column, the column of thousands, and so on.

Thus far we are carried along by the
stream, without the least trouble. Let us
now consider the 25 and 75 as fractional
parts of 100. In plainer terms, let us suppose a rod of any length you please, broken
into a hundred pieces; these pieces are properly called broken, or fractional, parts of
a hundred. But 25 being one fourth part
of 100, and 75 being three quarters of 100,
they might be thus written $\frac{1}{4}$ and $\frac{3}{4}$. How
are these two fractions to be added so as to
make a hundred?—The figure above the
line is called the *numerator*, because it indicates the number of parts, and the figure
below the line is called the *denominator*, because it denominates the kind of parts. In
these two fractions they are both of the same
denomination, both fourths: therefore, in
the

the prefent cafe, I have nothing to do but
to add the two numerators together for a
new numerator, and fubfcribe the common
denominator: the fraction will then ftand
thus $\frac{4}{4}$, that is, four fourths, equal to one
whole: four fourths of a hundred make a
hundred.

But fuppofe the fractions were $\frac{1}{4}$ and $\frac{5}{8}$,
I cannot add them together until I have
brought them to the fame denomination:
that is, until their denominators are alike;
eighths and fourths cannot be accumulated
in one homogeneous fum. I confider that
in multiplying feparately any two figures
by any one other figure, I neither increafe
nor diminifh their relative value; for, if I
double, that is, if I multiply by 2, the two
figures which I will fuppofe to fignify the
half of a fhilling, viz. $\frac{1}{2}$, the 1 becomes a 2
and the 2 a 4, thus $\frac{2}{4}$. Now one half of a
fhilling is fix pence, and two fourths are twice
three pence:—hence, I firft quadruple, that
is, multiply the two figures of the fecond fraction by 4, the denominator of the firft, and the
product is $\frac{24}{32}$. I then multiply both the
figures of the firft fraction by 8, the denominator of the fecond, and find the product $\frac{8}{32}$.
Thus I have brought them to one denomi-
nation;

nation; fo that I can now add the numerators 24 and 8: the fum is 32 for a new numerator: my fraction therefore thus added
is $\frac{32}{32}$ equal to one whole, or one hundred:
for all the parts of any thing muft be equal
to the whole. This may be made ftill plainer,
thus. Without any knowledge of Euclid,
or of Arithmetic, a moment's reflexion con-
vinces me, that, if I take equal quantities
from any two numbers, their proportion to
each other will remain the fame: fo that if
I take half from the $\frac{32}{32}$ there will remain
$\frac{16}{16}$. If I then take half from each of thefe
fixteens, there will remain $\frac{8}{8}$. One ftep farther brings the fraction to $\frac{4}{4}$; the next ftep
to $\frac{2}{2}$ and the laft to $\frac{1}{1}$, which is evidently
the fame as *one* a whole number; for one
ones is one.

Let us now confider, whether it be not
poffible to manage this 25, the quarter, and
this 75, the three quarters, of a hundred,
without being troubled with thefe denominators beneath the line? You know I firft
wrote them thus $\frac{1}{4}$ and $\frac{3}{4}$. But if for the 1
I fubftitute 25, and for the three I take 75,
I muft then write $\frac{25}{100}$ and $\frac{75}{100}$. You remember, that thefe denominators, thefe un-
der figures, indicate the fpecies of parts:

F   they

they tell us, in the prefent cafe, that the 25 and 75 are parts of a hundred. Knowing therefore what they are, I can add them, fubtract them one from the other, or work with them in any manner I pleafe, juft as I would with whole numbers. But before I difcover to you what I am about, another previous ftep is neceffary.

Imagine that I have before me the fraction $\frac{1}{2}$. I want to exprefs its value by a fingle figure, without this troublefome denominator. I know that I can multiply thefe two figures feparately by any other figure without altering their value, thus multiplying them by 5, the 1 becomes a 5 and the 2 a 10: the fraction therefore is now $\frac{5}{10}$ or $\frac{50}{100}$ or $\frac{500}{1000}$. I now perceive that I have no farther occafion for thefe denominators; that in thefe Decimal Fractions *one* figure denotes tenths, *two* figures hundredths, *three* figures thoufandths: thus ,4 with a comma before it, fignifies four parts of ten; ,37 means thirty feven parts of a hundred; ,365, are three hundred and fixty five parts of a thoufand. This being perfectly underftood, I can add thefe Decimals in the fame manner as whole numbers. For example,

To

To ,74. I proceed as in common Addition. Add ,39

The fum is 113. What is this fum? Why it is a 113 hundredth parts; for, there being only two figures in either of the Decimals, it is evident, that when added together, the fum muft neceffarily confift of hundredths. But 113 hundredth parts make one entire hundred and 13 fractional parts of another hundred. The 1 therefore on the left hand ceafes to be a fraction: it becomes what Arithmeticians call an Integer; that is, a whole number: fo that I muft point it thus 1,13. Hence the rule that in the addition of Decimals *you muft point off as many figures as there are figures in either of the numbers to be added.*

This rule you will find in all books of Arithmetic; but the authors of thefe books never give any reafon for the rule; it becomes therefore a mere matter of memory and is foon forgotten.

The ten figures ufed in vulgar and decimal Arithmetic are doubtlefs wonderful inftruments for the purpofe of calculation. Let us try however whether it be not poffible to find other fymbols, which, by figni-

fying

fying any fum at pleafure, may render calculation lefs laborious.

Suppofe, for example, the letter *b* repre-
fents 750l. If I have two creditors, each of
which owe me exactly this fum, and I want
to know the whole amount, according to
the rules of addition in common Arithmetic, I proceed in this manner 750

$$\begin{array}{r} 750 \\ \underline{750} \\ 1500. \end{array}$$

But fup-
pofing the letter *b* to reprefent 750l. I then
place the two fymbols under each other,
thus

$$\begin{array}{l} \text{To} \quad b \\ \text{Add} \quad \underline{b} \end{array}$$

The fum is $\underline{2b}$, equal to 1500l.

This Science, in which letters are ufed inftead of figures, is called *Algebra*, a word
derived from the Arabic *al-giabr wolmokabala*,
fignifying, *the art of refolution and equation.*
It is fuppofed to have been invented in India, and that the Arabs received it from the
Perfians. It is certain however that it was
brought into Europe by the Moors, who
conquered Spain in the 8th century. The
firft printed book in Algebra was written

by

by Lucas de Burgo, and publifhed at Venice, in the year 1494. You will be infinitely pleafed and aftonifhed at the power of this Science, when you become perfectly acquainted with its ufe. I am in this letter, fpeaking only of the various modes of Addition, viz. of figures as fymbols of whole numbers, of vulgar fractions, of decimal fractions, and of letters as fymbols of number or quantity.

But, before we proceed with the addition of thefe Algebraic quantities, I muft tell you, that Algebraifts fuppofe every quantity, or letter, to be either *pofitive*, of which this $+$ is their fign; or negative, which they mark thus $-$. The firft they read *plus*, the other *minus*. You muft alfo remember, that when there is no fign prefixed, *plus* is always underftood, and that when there is no figure before the letter or quantity, the figure 1 is fuppofed.

(1)	(2)	(3)	(4)
To 3*a*	To $-$ *b*	To $-$ 9*x*	To $+$7*y*
Add *a*	Add $-$2*b*	Add $+$12*x*	Add $-$9*y*
Sum 4*a*	$-$3*b*	$+$ 3*x*	$-$2*y*

(5)

(5)

$$\begin{aligned}
&\text{To } \quad 2c + 3b - 7x \\
&\text{Add} \quad 4z - 6y + b \\
\hline
&\text{Sum } 2c + 3b - 7x + 4z - 6y + b
\end{aligned}$$

The truth of the firſt example is very obvious. Suppoſe a to repreſent any poſitive quantity, once a added to three times a muſt make four times a.

In the ſecond example, the quantities are both negative: they repreſent a want or deficiency. Now a want of one ſhilling added to a want of 2 ſhillings, amounts to a want of 3 ſhillings, or $-3b$.

But in example the third, the ſigns are different. How is it poſſible to add a poſitive to a negative quantity? It is impoſſible; but it is very evident, that by taking one out of the other; that is, by ſubtracting the leſs from the greater, I ſhall diſcover the amount: for, if I have 12 ſhillings in my pocket, and owe you 9, which 9 is, to me, a negative quantity, I have yet a poſitive 3 ſhillings remaining; therefore the amount of my ſtock and debt taken together, may be properly expreſſed by $+3x$. This, I confeſs, is a ſpecies of Iriſh Addition, performed by Subtraction: it is, nevertheleſs,

con-

confidered as an operation of Addition in all the books of Algebra.

In the fourth example the figns are again diffimilar; but here the negative fum exceeds the pofitive. No matter: I fubtract the lefs from the greater, as in the former example, and to the remainder 2, I prefix the fign of *minus*; for, if I owe you 9 fhillings and can pay you only 7, there is a deficiency of 2, properly expreffed by $-2y$.

In contemplating the fifth example, I immediately perceive, that there are no two quantities alike; and, as I am ignorant what thefe feveral letters, or quantities, may fignify, it is impoffible to add them by any other means, than by writing them down in fucceffion with their refpective figns, as in the under-written fum.

If you take the trouble to read this letter a fecond time, with any degree of attention, you will not only comprehend the nature of Addition of whole numbers, vulgar and decimal fractions and of Algebraic quantities; but you will have acquired a general idea of thefe feveral modes of computation. This general idea will confiderably facilitate your progrefs in mathematical learning.

 L E T-

LETTER XI.

IN my laft letter, I endeavoured to give you a clear idea of the feveral contrivances for the addition, or accumulation, of numbers or quantities. They are all founded on the fame principle; their object is the fame, and, being thus linked together, mutually illuftrating each other, feem moft likely to imprefs the mind fcientifically. I fhall now proceed to SUBTRACTION, the *rationale* of which you will eafily comprehend. The defign of this operation is, by taking a lefs number from a greater, to difcover the difference. For example,

From 769
Take 436

Sum 333

Beginning with the firft figure on the right, I fay 6 from 9 there remains 3; then 3 from 6, there remains 3; and laftly, 4 from 7 and the remainder is 3. To prove that I am right, I add the *fum* to the lefs of the two numbers above, and find, that together, they make 769.

Again;

Again: From 9312
　　　Take 7434
　　　Sum 1878

If you were totally ignorant of the firſt rules of Arithmetic, you would not immediately diſcover by what means 4 could be ſubtraƐted from 2, or 3 from 1, or again 4 from 3. But, if in your mind, you take ten from the next figure and add it to the 2, you can then ſubtraƐt the 4 from 12 and the remainder will be 8.—You now proceed to the next figure 3, which you are to ſubtraƐt from the 1 above it, but as you have already taken 10 from this 1, which ſtanding in the ten's place is one ten, it becomes a 0; therefore you are to ſubtraƐt 3 from 0: this being impoſſible, you again take ten from the next figure and ſubtraƐting 3 from ten, you put down 7. You are now to take 4 from the 3 above; but this 3 is, in faƐt, only 2, for the ſame reaſon that the 1 became a 0; 4 cannot be ſubtraƐted from 2; I therefore take ten from the 9000, and ſay 4 from 12, there remains 8. But you are to obſerve, though I call it taking *ten* from the next figure, that, when from the 3 I took 10, in faƐt I took 100; properly

ſpeak-fpeaking, therefore, I fhould have faid, 30 from 0 is impoffible; but 30 from 100, there remains 70. In like manner, the 10 which I took from the 9, was in reality 1000: fo that in taking 4 from 12, I was really fub-tracting 400 from 1200.—You now pro-ceed to the 7, and, recollecting that one of the thoufands was ufed among the hun-dreds, you fay 7 from 8, or rather 7000 from 8000, there remains 1000.

You will probably think that I have been unneceffarily minute in a matter of little importance. Nothing is unimportant that may throw a fingle ray of light on the threfhold of Science. I am thus explicit on the *Subtraction* of whole numbers, becaufe the manner in which it is taught in our fchools, feems particularly defigned to pre-vent the boys from conceiving any more than a mechanical idea of the operation: or, if they have any other idea at all, it is certainly falfe. They are inftructed to bor-row *ten* from the next figure in the upper line, which ten they afterwards call *one* and reftore it to the next figure in the under line. Now, though the refult be the fame, whether I increafe the lower, or diminifh the upper line, by *one*, why miflead the

learner

learner by a falſe operation? why uſe the improper term *borrow?* It implies the neceſſity of reſtoration. But, in fact, there is nothing borrowed, and conſequently nothing to be reſtored. What is taken from the next figure, is taken abſolutely and uſed: it has already, prematurely, yielded its ſubtractive part, and therefore is not liable to a ſecond diminution: The figure from which it was taken, if it ſtand in the 2d place from the right, has loſt ten of its value; if in the 3d it has loſt a 100: ſo that if the figure be a 7, I conſider it as a 6, and act accordingly.

I now proceed to give you a general notion of ſubtracting *fractional* numbers from each other. If, for example, you were required to take $\frac{1}{4}$ from $\frac{3}{4}$, it is very evident that the remainder will be $\frac{2}{4}$, or $\frac{1}{2}$: ſo that when the denominators are the ſame, you have nothing to do, but to ſubtract the leſs numerator from the greater.

If the denominators be not the ſame, reduce them to fractions of the ſame denomination, by multiplying each numerator into the other's denominator for two new numerators, and the denominators by each other, for a common denominator; then proceed

as

as in the laft example, thus: Suppofe the two fractions to be $\frac{7}{8}$ and $\frac{3}{5}$; reduced to the fame denomination, they become $\frac{35}{40}$ and $\frac{24}{40}$; the numerators of which being fubtracted from each other, the remaining fraction is $\frac{11}{40}$.

You remember that, in thefe vulgar fractions, the under figure tells you the parts into which the upper figure is fuppofed to be divided, and the upper figure indicates the number of thefe parts: the denominator therefore is confidered as the *devifor* and the numerator as the *dividend*, But you will afk, how can a lefs number be divided by a greater, a 7 by 8, or 3 by 5, or 1 by 2? —Would you find any difficulty in cutting this orange in two? No—Well: What are thefe two pieces?—They are two halves. Then it is evident that 1 orange may be divided into, or by, 2, and that $\frac{1}{2}$ would exprefs one of thefe halves: to halve a number therefore is to divide it by 2.

But to render this numerator 1 actually divifible by the denominator 2, let us fuppofe it to confift of ten equal parts: we therefore add a cypher to it and call it 10 parts inftead of 1 whole number. I now write the fraction $\frac{10}{2}$; that is, 10 divided by

2; and, proceeding to divide the numerator by the denominator, by afking how often 2 in 10 tenths, the anfwer is 5 tenths; which 5 having 10 for its denominator, I call a decimal fraction. So that the way to reduce a vulgar fraction to a decimal, I find, is to add a cypher to the numerator and divide by the denominator. If I had added two cyphers and divided by 2, the product would have been ,50 that is, 50 parts of 100; equal to 5 parts of 10; equal to $\frac{1}{2}$ or 1 divided by 2.

According to this rule, let us reduce $\frac{3}{5}$ to a decimal fraction. Adding one cypher to the 3 it becomes 30, and dividing 30 by 5 the anfwer is 6, that is $\frac{6}{10}$ which being a decimal, I write thus ,6. So the vulgar fraction $\frac{1}{2}$ reduced to a decimal is ,5, and $\frac{3}{5}$ is ,6. This 5 may be fubtracted from the 6, as in fubtraction of whole numbers, and the remainder is ,1; that is, one tenth: for as both the 5 and 6 are tenth parts of an unit, the remaining 1 muft necessarily be $\frac{1}{10}$ of an unit.

Let us now confider the Subtraction of Algebraic quantities. This is the Rule. *Reverfe the figns of the quantity to be fubtracted and proceed as in Addition:* for example,

$$
\begin{array}{ll}
(1) & \\
\text{From } 3\,a & \\
\text{Take }\ \ a & \\
\hline
\ \ 2\,a &
\end{array}
\qquad
\begin{array}{ll}
(2) & \\
\text{From} -2\,b & \\
\text{Take} -\ b & \\
\hline
\ -\ b &
\end{array}
\qquad
\begin{array}{ll}
(3) & \\
\text{From} -12\,x & \\
\text{Take }\ \ 9\,x & \\
\hline
\ -21\,x &
\end{array}
$$

$$
\begin{array}{l}
(4) \\
\text{From }\ \ 9\,y \\
\text{Take} -7\,y \\
\hline
\ \ 16\,y
\end{array}
$$

In the firſt and ſecond of theſe examples, the ſigns, in both quantities, are alike: but, if I ſuppoſe the ſign of the ſufttrahend to be reverſed, they are then oppoſite. Now the rule in Addition is, *when the ſigns are not the ſame, ſubtract the leſs from the greater, and put down the remainder with the ſign of the greater*: hence a from $3\,a$, and the remainder is $2\,a$. In like manner $-b$ from $-2\,b$, there remains $-b$.

In the third and fourth examples, the ſigns are oppoſite; but ſuppoſing the ſigns of the ſubtrahends to be reverſed, they will then become ſimilar to thoſe of the quantities above them: I have therefore nothing to do but to add the figures, (which are called Coefficients,) as in common Arithmetic, prefixing the common ſign of both.

Thus

Thus it appears, that Subtraction differs from Addition only in reverſing the ſigns of the ſubtrahend.

This is all very true. Theſe are the rules which you will find in the elementary books of Algebra. But this confounding Subtraction with Addition, ſerves only to jumble the ideas of the learner. The following general rule is ſufficient both for Addition and Subtraction.

In Addition, *when the ſigns are the ſame,* ADD; *when they are oppoſite,* SUBTRACT. In Subtraction, *when the ſigns are the ſame,* SUBTRACT; *when oppoſite,* ADD. This rule being obſerved, you proceed naturally, without any ſuppoſed change of ſigns. The reaſons for the three firſt parts of this Rule are ſelf-evident: the laſt requires explanation. I have ſaid, that, in Subtraction, when the ſigns are oppoſite, that is, when one is $+$ and the other $-$, you are to add the co-efficients. How, you will aſk, will this addition be in reality a ſubtraction. I will firſt prove the fact, and then account for it.

From $10\,a - 56$ To $10\,a - 56$
Take $- 56$ Add $+ 56$
─────────────   ─────────────
$10\,a$ $10\,a$

In

In both cafes you fee the remainder is the fame. Suppofe, by way of illuftration, after a ballot, I find in the bag 10 white balls and 5 black ones. If I take out the black balls, there will remain 10 white balls in the bag. But if before I take out any of the balls, I put in 5 white ones, and then take out the 5 black balls with the fame number of white ones to ballance them, there will remain in the bag 10 white balls as before. Or fuppofe you were five pounds in my debt, and that you are worth nothing, you are then five pounds worfe than nothing. Your cafh account is — 5 pounds. But if any friend fhould pay the debt, by thus adding his + five pounds to your — five pounds, he actually fubtracts your debt: fo that, in this cafe, addition and fubtraction are the fame.

LETTER XII.

I SUPPOSE you have not forgotten your Multiplication-table. If you have it not quite perfect, fpend half an hour in giving it a firm eftablifhment in your memory; for the leaft miftake or hefitation in the mechanical part of multiplication, will leave a bad impreffion on the mind of your Tutor.

The operation of multiplying one row of figures by another, is eafily learnt, but not generally underftood. I will endeavour to explain it by a fhort example. It is neceffary however, previoufly to obferve, that Multiplication and Addition are in reality the fame: thus,

$$\text{Add} \quad \left\{\begin{array}{l} 3 \\ 3 \\ 3 \end{array}\right.$$

$$\text{Sum} \quad . \quad \underline{9}$$

$$\begin{array}{ll} \text{Multiply} & 3 \\ \text{by} \quad . & \underline{3} \\ \text{Product} & \underline{9} \end{array}$$

G   The

The *modus operandi* in Multiplication is as follows.

Multiply 425
by   .   213
———————
1275
425
850
———————
90525
———————

In the above example, beginning with the first figure on the right hand, I say, in the common language of the school, 3 times 5 is 15, put down 5 and carry 1; 3 times 2 is 6, and 1 that I brought is 7; 3 times 4 is 12, put down 12. I then take the second figure, from the right, of the *multiplier*, and with it multiply all the figures of the *multiplicand* as before, putting down the product in a second line, taking care to place the first figure under the second figure of the first line. I then proceed in the same manner with the third figure of the multiplier, placing the first figure of the result under the third of the first product; as you see in the example. The separate results of these three multiplications being thus arranged beneath each other, I add them together and the sum is the product of the
whole

whole multiplication. This may be all very true: the method of multiplying, of carrying *one* to the next figure, of arranging the feveral rows inclining gradually to the left — may be rational, but the reafon is not very apparent. Let us try to explain the operation and demonftrate the truth of the refult.

I am to multiply 425
by 213
———

Firft, I fay, 3 times 5 make .	15
Secondly, 3 times 20 make .	60
Thirdly, 3 times 400 make .	1200

I now begin to work with the figure
1: remembering it is a *ten*,

I fay, ten times 5 make . .	50
Then, ten times 20 make . .	200
And ten times 400 make . .	4000

I now multiply with the figure 2, remembering that it is 200: thus

200 times 5 make . .	1000
Secondly, 200 times 20 make .	4000
Laftly, 200 times 400 make .	80000

Now thefe added together make .	90525

as before: fo that the ufual concife method of Multiplication is demonftrably true.

From the foregoing example it is impof-

      fible

fible not to underftand the *rationale* of mul*
tiplying whole numbers: the multiplication
of fractions is equally eafy and intelligible.
For example, Multiply $\frac{2}{3}$ by $\frac{3}{4}$.   The rule
is, *multiply the numerators for a new numerator
and the denominators for a new denominator:*
thus—twice 3 are 6, and 3 times 4 are 12:
the fraction will be $\frac{6}{12}$ or $\frac{2}{4}$ or $\frac{1}{2}$.

To prove the truth of this operation, we
will fuppofe thefe fractions to be parts of a
fhilling, or pence.   Now, two thirds of a
fhilling are 8 pence, and three fourths of a
fhilling are 9 pence: 8 times 9 make 72 pence;
that is $\frac{72}{12}$ or parts of a fhilling.   But recollecting that I can reduce this fraction to
one of equal value by dividing the numerator and denominator by the fame number, I divide them by 6, and then fubftitute
$\frac{12}{2}$, that is, 12 divided by 2: but to divide a
number by 2, is to halve that number; fo that
the refult is $\frac{1}{2}$ of a fhilling or 6 pence, the
fame as above.

The Multiplication of Decimals differs
not in the leaft from that of whole numbers,
except that, in the product, you are to point
off as many figures as there are decimals in
the multiplier and multiplicand; thus,

2,97

$$2,97$$
$$3,6$$
$$\overline{1782}$$
$$891$$
$$\overline{10,692}$$

There being two decimals in the multiplicand and one in the multiplier, I point off three decimals in the product.

In the multiplication of Algebraic quantities, you have only to write the letters in a line one after the other; to multiply the coefficients as in common Arithmetic, and, when the figns are fimilar, to prefix the fign $+$, when diffimilar $-$, thus,

Multiply a	Multiply $-c$	Multiply $-d$
By b	By $-d$	By $+e$
Product ab	$+cd$	$-de$

Multiply $12x$
By $\quad -3y$
$\overline{-36xy}$

Multiply $x+y$
By $\quad x+y$
$\overline{xx+xy}$
$\quad\quad xy+yy$
$\overline{xx+2xy+yy}$

This, you will fay, is very eafy and perfectly clear, as to the manner of working: but

you

you will not, without a little reflection, difcover the reafon why, when the figns of the
multiplier and multiplicand, are different,
you are always to prefix the negative fign
to the product. I will endeavour to explain
this matter.

Pofitive and negative quantities are confidered as diametrically oppofite. If from
a given point I draw a line to the right, I
may call it pofitive; then a line from the
fame point, drawn to the left, may be confidered as a negative line. Or, if I place a
cypher in the middle and continue a line of
figures both ways, thus 4321 o 1234, thofe
on the right are *more* than nothing; thofe on
the left I will imagine *lefs*. The firft may
exprefs money which I poffefs, the latter,
money which I owe. Let us fuppofe, for
example, that I find, in three different parts
of my account-book, a debt of 15 l. which
I have borrowed of a friend.

I exprefs it thus . . . —15:
   and finding it three time repeated, I multiply by . . + 3:
   that is, I tripple the debt, and
   confequently the product is . —45.

If, on the contrary, I fuppofe this 15 to
repre-

reprefent all the guineas in my purfe, I
write it thus . . . $+15.$
But I owe 3 times 15 guineas; I
therefore prefix the negative fign $-3.$

And the product is . . $-45,$

as before:

Now fuppofing the letter *a* to ftand for 15
guineas, the real ftate of my account may
be thus algebraically reprefented . . .
$a-3a=-30.$ That is, I am 30 guineas
worfe than nothing. In both cafes the propriety of prefixing the negative fign is evident, becaufe the product is really a defect.
In multiplying a negative quantity, or deficiency, or debt, I am adding it to itfelf as
often as there are units in the multiplier. I
thus increafe the debt, but I do not thereby
alter its nature: it ftill remains a debt, and
therefore retains its negative fign. To underftand the other cafe, viz. when a pofitive
quantity is multiplied by a negative, it is
neceffary to recollect, that to multiply my
debts, is in fact, to fubtract from my real
fubftance; therefore, though I work by
multiplication, when the multiplier has the
negative fign, I am actually fubtracting the
multiplicand from reality; that is, reducing

it

it below nothing, as many times as there are units in the multiplier; therefore the product muſt neceſſarily be a negative quantity.

But you will aſk, what is the reaſon that when two negative quantities are multiplied by each other, the product muſt have a poſitive ſign? The reaſon is plain: for, if to multiply by a negative quantity be to ſubtract, then ſuch multiplication is actually ſubtracting from the Debtor page of my account-book, which has the ſame effect as if the ſum were added to the Creditor ſide. To ſubtract *minus* is the ſame thing as to add *plus*. If I diſcharge, or take away your debt of a guinea at the fruit-ſhop, it is certainly equivalent to my giving you a guinea. But before I conclude this introduction to Multiplication — for it is no more than an introduction — it is neceſſary to obſerve, that the multiplier, whether it be a poſitive or a negative quantity, or, whatſoever it may be called, is always nothing more than a number, without any real denomination. A pound cannot be multiplied by a pound, nor a mile by a mile.

L E T-

LETTER XIII.

IN this letter I mean to call your attention to the Divifion of whole numbers,
fractions, and of algebraical quantities. As
Subtraction is the reverfe of Addition, fo is
Divifion the reverfe of Multiplication. But
we have feen that Multiplication is really a
compendious Addition, and you will foon
perceive, that Divifion is nothing more than
a method of determining, how many times
a lefs number is contained in, or may be
fubtracted from, a greater; fo that all the
various operations of Arithmetic, are in fact,
Additions or Subtractions. For example,

$$
\text{Add}\begin{cases} 5 \\ 5 \\ 5 \\ 5 \\ 5 \\ 5 \\ 5 \\ 5 \end{cases}
\qquad
\begin{array}{r}
\text{Multiply } 5 \\
\text{By} \quad 7 \\
\hline
\text{Product } 35 \\
\hline
\end{array}
\qquad
\begin{array}{r}
\text{From } 7 \\
\text{Take } 5 \\
\hline
\text{Remains } 2 \\
\hline
\end{array}
$$

$$
\text{Sum } 35
\qquad\qquad
\begin{array}{r}
5)\,7\,(1 \\
5 \\
\hline
2 \\
\hline
\end{array}
$$

In the fourth of thefe examples, the 5 on
the left is called the *divifor*, the 7 is the *di-*
vidend,

vidend, the 1 is the *quotient*, and the 2, the *remainder*. But that you may fee the whole operation of Divifion, we will take an example of more figures.

Divide 7634 by 8. I difpofe thefe two numbers thus

$$8)\,7634\,(954$$
$$\underline{72}$$
$$43$$
$$\underline{40}$$
$$34$$
$$\underline{32}$$
$$2.$$

I begin by afking, how many times 8 is contained in 76? Recollecting that 9 times 8 make 72, I write 9 in the quotient and 72 under 76, which 72 I fubtract from 76, and drawing a line acrofs, I write under it the remainder 4, to which I bring down the figure 3 from the dividend. I now afk, how often 8 in 43? 5 times 8 make 40, which being fubtracted from 43, there remains 3. To this 3 I annex the laft figure of the dividend. I then afk, how often 8 in 34? 4 times 8 is 32: I therefore write 4 in the quotient, and fubtracting 32 from 34, the remainder is 2.

Hence,

Hence, I learn, that from the number 7634, 8 may be fubtracted 954 times, and there will remain a furplus of 2.—What is this 2? It is a fraction. It is $\frac{2}{8}$. But to render this more intelligible, let us fuppofe 7634 to be fo many pounds fterling bequeathed to be equally divided among 8 Legatees: the quotient tells me, that they are entitled to 954£. each, and $\frac{2}{8}$; that is, two eighths of a pound: this remainder therefore muft be multiplied by 20 in order to reduce it to fhillings. The product is 40, which being divided by 8, gives 5: fo that each Legatee will receive 954£. 5s. —

I have faid that Divifion is the reverfe of Multiplication. We will put this affertion to the proof by trying to rebuild, by the laft, what, by the firft, we have pulled down. If 8 be contained 954 times in 7634, then the firft of thefe two numbers multiplied by 8, with the addition of the remainder 2, muft pruduce the laft.

```
Multiply     954
By      .      8
            ______
             7632
Add     .       2
            ______
             7634
```

This

This product proves, not only that Multiplication and Divifion are the reverfe of each other; but that the Quotient was juft.

According to the plan I have obferved in Addition, Subtraction, and Multiplication, we now proceed to the Divifion of Vulgar Fractions. Firft, let us try to divide a fraction by a whole number.

Divide $\frac{6}{7}$ by 3. Now a moment's reflection tells me, that I have nothing to do with the denominator, which is put not to indicate the *number* but the *kind* of parts: therefore I muft divide the numerator 6 by 3 and the quotient will be $\frac{2}{7}$. We will, by way of illuftration, fuppofe this denominator to indicate parts of a guinea. Now, 7 times 3 is 21; therefore, one feventh of a guinea is 3 fhillings: 6 times 3 make 18; therefore $\frac{6}{7}$ of a guinea are 18 fhillings, that is, $\frac{18}{21}$. I now afk, how often 3 fhillings in 18. The anfwer is 6 fhillings or $\frac{2}{7}$ of a guinea.

Let us now try to divide a fraction by a fraction.

For example, Divide $\frac{2}{3}$ by $\frac{2}{3}$.

This is the rule: *Multiply the Numerator of the Dividend by the Denominator of the Divifor, for a new Numerator, and the Denomina-*

tor

tor of the Dividend by the Numerator of the Divisor, for a new Denominator. Let us place thefe two fractions as in common divifion and try $\frac{2}{3})\frac{5}{7}(\frac{15}{14}.$

There is yet a fhorter and a plainer rule, viz. *Reverfe one of the fractions; then multiply the two numerators and the two denominators:* thus $\frac{3}{2})\frac{5}{7}(\frac{15}{14}$

The quotient, I find, is 15 divided by 14. But why this *multiplication* fhould be, in fact, *divifion*, is by no means obvious: nor do I recollect any author who explains it fufficiently. Firft, let us confider, that *fevenths* cannot be divided into *thirds:* therefore, fuppofe I had never heard of any rule for dividing one fraction by another, I fhould naturally begin by multiplying the numerators and denominators reciprocally, for two new numerators; and the denominators, for a common denominator: the refult of which operation would be $\frac{15}{21}$, $\frac{14}{21}$. Now all the difficulty is vanifhed. Since the denominators are the fame, they become ufelefs, and I can add, fubtract, multiply, or divide the numerators in the fame manner as if they were whole numbers. Now as $\frac{15}{21}$ is equivalent to the dividend, and $\frac{14}{21}$ equal to the divifor, the quotient muft be $\frac{15}{14}$.

But

But all this does not explain the rule: for you see that we have done without it. The rule, you know, is, to multiply the numerators by the denominators reciprocally. Now what is this, but reducing the two fractions to one denomination, and then dividing the greater numerator by the lefs? So that after all, this multiplication is merely the inftrument for reducing the two fractions to a common denomination, and not an actual divifion.

But to prove that our quotient is juft, we will try whether, when multiplied by the divifor, the product will be the dividend.

$$\frac{15}{2} \quad \frac{14}{3} \qquad \frac{30}{42} = \frac{10}{14} = \frac{5}{7} \quad \text{Q. E. D.}$$
$$\frac{2}{30} \quad \frac{3}{42}$$

The Divifion of Decimal Fractions differs from the divifion of whole numbers only in the art of pointing off the figures in the quotient: and the rule is—Point off in the quotient as many figures, counting from the right hand, as the number of decimals in the dividend exceeds thofe in the divifor. In other words: the number of decimals in the quotient and divifor, muft together, equal the number of thofe in the dividend:

con-

confequently, when the number of decimal figures in the divifor and dividend is equal, the quotient will be whole numbers.

$$4,2)612,318(145,79$$

$$
\begin{array}{r}
42 \\
\hline
192 \\
168 \\
\hline
\cdot 243 \\
210 \\
\hline
331 \\
294 \\
\hline
\cdot 378 \\
378 \\
\hline
\end{array}
$$

In the dividend there are 3 decimal figures; in the divifor, but one: therefore, according to the above rule, I point off two figures in the quotient for decimals, the reft being whole numbers.

We come now to the Divifion of Algebraic quantities.

Firft, you are to remember that (as in Multiplication) fimilar figns give + and diffimilar — in the quotient. *Secondly*, that when fimilar quantities occur both in the divifor and in the dividend, thefe quantities

may

may be expunged. *Thirdly*, that the quotient is generally expreffed by placing the
dividend above and the divifor beneath a
line drawn between them, as in vulgar fractions. *Fourthly*, that coefficients are to be
divided as in common Arithmetic; or divided by a common meafure.

$$20ad\overline{)}15ac\left(\dfrac{3d+c}{4d}\right.$$

In this example, I have divided the coefficients by 5 and expunged the letter *a*.
The reafon for dividing the figures by a
common meafure is felf-evident, and the
reafon for expunging this letter *a* will be no
lefs obvious when you recollect, that letters,
or quantities, thus written next to each
other, as *ad* and *ac*, are fuppofed to be multiplied one by the other; and that, in vulgar
fractions, the numerator and denominator,
that is, the dividend and divifor, being multiplied or divided by the fame number,
makes no alteration in their ralative value.
But, to render this matter more intelligible,
let us fuppofe *ac*, the dividend, to reprefent
4 multiplied by 6, and *ad*, the divifor, to
mean 4 multiplied by 2: now 4 times 6
make 24, and twice 4 is 8. If I divide 24
by 8 the quotient is 3. But if I take 4, of
which

which *a* is the reprefentative, from both, the dividend will be 6, and the divifor 2. I then fay, how often 2 in 6? the anfwer is 3, as before.

As to the Divifion of Algebraical Fractions, it is performed, as in Vulgar Fractions, by multiplying the numerators and denominators reciprocally, thus

$$\left.\frac{c}{d}\right)\frac{a}{b}\left(\frac{ad}{cb}\right. \qquad \left.\frac{a+b}{a-b}\right)\frac{a-b}{a}\left(\frac{a^2-2ab+b^2}{a^2+ab}\right.$$

The fecond example requires explanation. I begin by multiplying the Denominator of the Divifor by the Numerator of the Dividend, thus: *a* multiplied by *a* produces *aa*; I write, in the product, one *a* with a fmall figure of two over it, which figure is called its index, fignifying the fecond power of *a*, or the product of *a* multiplied by *a*. I then multiply the fame $+a$ by $-b$, and $-b$ by $+a$, both which produce *ab*, and the figns being diffimilar, I put down in the dividend of the quotient $-2ab$: finally $-b$ multiplied by $-b$ gives $+b^2$. I now multiply the numerator of the divifor by the denominator of the dividend, and the product is evidently the denominator of the quotient.

Thus, I have endeavoured to give you a rational idea of Addition, Subtraction, Mul-

H

tiplication

tiplication and Divifion of whole numbers, fractions vulgar and decimal, and of Algebraic quantities. I fay a *rational* idea, diftinguifhed from the mechanical fyftem of introduction, which you will find in the elementary books. What I have done is nothing more than a partial explanation, or analyfis, of the machines with which you are to work: a tolerable comprehenfion of their conftruction, cannot fail to facilitate your future labours.

Vale.

LETTER XIV.

YOU are certainly right, I had forgotten that, in a former letter, I promised to introduce you to the acquaintance of the philofopher Ariftotle. I will now fulfil that promife, to the beft of my recollection.

ARISTOTLE flourifhed about three hundred years prior to the Chriftian *æra*. He was born in a fmall town in Macedonia named *Stagira*, and thence he is often called the *Stagirite*. Plato, Demofthenes, and the great Alexander, were his cotemporaries. Of the firft he was the pupil, and the preceptor of the laft. He is generally regarded as the founder of the Peripatetic fect of Philofophers; though fome hiftorians tell us, that the denomination originated in Plato, who, it feems, was as fond of ambulatory ftudies as myfelf: indeed thofe who ftudy Nature, will make no very rapid progrefs *fub tecto*. They were called *Peripatetics* from περιπατεω, *ambulo*, to diftinguifh them from the difciples of Xenocrates, who affumed the name of *Academics*, becaufe they affembled, at Athens, in the *Academy*; whilft

 the

the Peripatetics *walked* in the *Lyceum*. From this fcrap of Grecian hiftory, I fuppofe, the Artifts in London, when they quarrelled with their brethren of the Royal Academy, dignified their room in the Strand, with the appellation of the *Lyceum*.

Whether thefe Peripatetics ftudied in company or alone, may admit of doubt fufficient to furnifh matter of difcuffion to a commentator on the Grecian hiftory: be the fact however as it might, I advife you fometimes to ftroll out without company. If you wifh to fix your ferious attention to any fubject of confequence; or, if you be particularly defirous of exerting, ftimulating and expanding your imagination, you will find more affiftance in the fields, from a genial atmofphere, a ferene fky, a fmiling landfcape, an extended horizon, than from the books on your table. I do not mean that you fhould become a *mifanthrope*; that you fhould always walk alone; far from it: chearful company is occafionally as neceffary to a ftudious man as the air he breaths. But, as I obferve that parties of frefhmen, in their walks, generally amufe themfelves with leaping over hedges and ditches, though fuch athletic fports may be very wholefome,

yet

yet I fhould think it not neceffary that every perambulation fhould be thus employed.

Ariftotle, we are told, wrote no lefs than four hundred books. If they were books of any fize; if they were even pamphlets, they can hardly have been worth reading. I believe, in general, thofe authors that have written *leaft*, have written beft. About twenty of thefe books are all that have efcaped the deftructive hand of Time, and the more relentlefs hand of Barbarifm. The fubjects on which they treat, are *ethics, poetry, logic, rhetoric, politics, phyfics,* and *metaphyfics.* But, as he wrote without fyftem, without data, without method, and without precifion, it is very difficult to afcertain his opinions: and what greatly adds to the uncertainty is, that his works have come down to us through the turbid medium of Latin tranflations from the Arabic, or Greek tranflations from the Latin.

Ariftotle appears, however, to have been the inventor of the art which we now call Logic, and of the fcience of Metaphyfics. His Ethics deferve but little praife. His Politics are prolix and obfcure: neverthelefs, we muft do him the juftice to acknowledge, that, though preceptor to the fon of

an

an abfolute prince, he had the refolution to devulge, and to reafon juftly on, the patriotic maxim, that *princes are elevated to dominion, not for their own advantage, but for the felicity of the people.* He defcribes the various forms of government then exifting; expofes their vices, and develops the caufes of their corruption.

His fyftem of Rhetoric is doubtlefs a work of genius, and the labour of a mind capable of minute difcrimination. His Logic is the Logic of every fucceeding age, and of the prefent day. His Phyfics, or Philofophy had no foundation. What he wrote, or rather what he is fuppofed to have written, upon Plants, is of very doubtful origin. But his book upon the Animal creation, is allowed to be genuine, and is indeed an aftonifhing performance. His anatomical and phyfiological defcriptions, muft have been the refult of innumerable diffections, unwearied affiduity, minute infpection, and great fagacity. He appears to have had no idea of fyftem or claffification. His work is a continued defcriptive comparifon of one animal with another, without a perfect identical defcription of any individual. The various fubjects which he diffected, and

whofe

whofe habits he fo well defcribes, were collected at a vaft expence, by order of his mu-
nificent and powerful pupil, prince, and patron, the conquerer of the then known
world.

His philofophical opinions are to be collected principally from his books *de Cælo*.
He confidered *matter*, *form* and *privation* as
the principles of all things, and this *matter*
he conceived to be eternal and indeftructible.
His *elements* are Fire, Air, Water and Earth.
Thefe have ftood their ground pretty well,
till difturbed by the chemical philofophy of
the prefent age, of which I may probably
tell you more another time. He denied the
annual and diurnal motion of the Earth,
which Pythagoras had afferted, and was
confequently weak enough to fuppofe that
the Sun, the Planets, and the fixed Stars; in
fhort, the whole vifible creation, turned
daily round this atom, which we call Earth.
Strange! that he fhould not allow common
fenfe to the Creator of the Univerfe, who
had given him fo great a fhare of human
underftanding.

When and where he died is not known;
but his philofophy lived and flourifhed univerfally till towards the end of the laft cen-

tury:

tury: being then gradually undermined by other philofophers, Des Cartes finally blew it up, whofe bafelefs fabric, as I told you before, was, in its turn, annihilated by Sir Ifaac Newton.

I faid above, that Ariftotle's fyftem of *Rhetoric* is a work of genius. It is an art which was formerly confidered as an indif-penfible branch of education in every part of Europe, and was accordingly taught, firft in the fchools, and afterwards purfued at the Univerfity, in Ariftotle's technical language and manner. It has however gradually fallen into difufe: neverthelefs, as fome of the technical terms of this art are retained, it is neceffary you fhould know their meaning; I will therefore apply the remaining part of this letter to the explanation of thofe terms which are moft neceffary to be underftood.

Rhetoric, from ρεω, *dico*, the Romans tranflated *Oratoria*; by which they underftood, the Art of fpeaking with effect; the Art of perfuafion. That it was an art in high efteem and cultivation among the Greeks, appears from Quintilian, who, I think, mentions upwards of twenty eminent profeffors of Rhetoric, in different parts of Greece.

The

The Romans, notwithstanding their eagerness to learn from their more polished neighbours the Greeks, were, at first, so apprehensive of the power of Oratory, that, by a decree of the Senate, they banished all Greek philosophers and rhetoricians. The prohibition, however, was of no long duration. Rhetoric was soon after studied and taught as an art, and Rome produced a Quintilian and a Cicero.

That some advantage may be derived from the study of Rhetoric, I have no doubt; but, that the great art of Persuasion is generally a boon from Nature, I am much more inclined to believe. The most fluent and most perspicuous speaker I ever heard, was a Leeds merchant, the brother of Mr. John Lee, a gentleman eminent at the bar, and, some time, Solicitor General. Yet this Mr. Thomas Lee probably had never read Aristotle, Quintilian, Longinus, nor any system of Rhetoric ancient or modern. We have at this time in both houses of Parliament, orators, scarce, if at all, inferior to those of Athens or Rome; yet these are more the pupils of Nature than of Art.

The purpose of Logic is, to convince; that of Rhetoric, to persuade; and this art

of

of perfuafion depends moft on a natural melodious tone of voice, a natural graceful-nefs of perfon and of action, a naturally expreffive and interefting form and difpofi-tion of features: by *interefting*, I rather mean what the French exprefs by the word *preve-nante*, for which we have no equivalent in our language — I fay, the power of an Ora-tor over his audience, will always depend, in a great degree, on that which art cannot beftow: neverthelefs, the beft gifts of nature want a little polifhing. I have heard fome eloquent members in the Houfe of Com-mons, who would have been much more perfuafive fpeakers, if they had ever learnt to dance: and though grammars, or fyftems of Rhetoric, may contribute nothing to the creation or embellifhment of a fine fpeaker; yet thofe who are intended for the pulpit, the bar, or have any profpect of a feat in Parliament, will gather much ufeful in-ftruction and improvement, from a careful and frequent reading of Longinus and Quin-tilian, and, for illuftration and example, Demofthenes and Cicero; nor fhould they neglect, in our own language, *Sheridan's Lectures on Elocution:* they contain a great deal of excellent matter.

As

As to artificial Logic, the Logic of the fchools, it is of no more ufe in polifhed difputation, than artificial Rhetoric to a polifhed Orator. One of the moft rational and powerful difputants I ever knew, was my late worthy friend Edward Gillyatt, of the Bank; yet he was totally ignorant of Logic, as an art. But, notwithftanding the inutility of thefe two arts, they are neceffary to be known by every gentleman who is not afhamed to acknowledge, that he has had the advantage of an Univerfity education. I will therefore give you a flight fketch of the art of Rhetoric, and an explanation of thofe terms of that art, which are moft neceffary to be underftood.

The Art of Rhetoric comprehends, Invention, Difpofition, Elocution and Pronunciation. As Grammar teaches the art of fpeaking properly, Rhetoric inftructs us how to fpeak with elegance and effect. The two great inftruments of this art, are Trope and Figure.

Trope, *Tropus*, τροπος from τρεπω, *muto*, literally means a change of one word for another: *eft vofis a proprio fignificatione in aliam immutatio.* It is a word ufed not in

its

its common acceptation, for the purpofe of adding power or beauty to the fentence. The *fpecies* of this *genus* are four, *viz.*

Metaphora, μεταφορα, from μετα, trans, and φερω, *fero.* It is a fimile expreffed in one word, thus—*You fhine a fcholar.*—*The tinkling of that rill is mufic.*—*That lad is a lion.*—*That girl is an angel.*—*Eft flos nobilitatis,* &c.

Metonymia, from μετα, and ονομα, *nomen,* a change of name: thus, when the caufe is put for the effect, as, *You fpeak the French tongue.* Or, the effect for the caufe, as in the firft Ode of Horace, *Præfidium et dulce decus meum.* Or, when the fubject is put for the adjunct: thus, *Roma pro Romanis, vel patera pro vino.*

Synecdoche, formed of συνεκδεχομαι, *comprendo,* takes the whole for a part, or part for the whole; as for example in the firft line of Milton's Paradife Loft:—"*Of man's firft difobedience and the fruit*"—Here *man* is taken for *mankind:* fo when the Latin poets ufe *aufter* for *wind;* or *falernum* for *wine* in general. In thefe examples, the *fpecies* is taken for the *genus,* or the individual for the

fpecies.

fpecies. On the contrary, the clafs is taken for the *genus* by Virgil when he fays — *tollit fe arrectum quadrupes.*

Ironia — *diffimulatio, illufio, diverfiloquium,* means the reverfe of that which is exprefled: thus Terence — *ebodum, bone vir!*

Thefe are confidered, by Rhetoricians, as the four primary Tropes, which they fubdivide into a number of *fpecies*; or to fpeak more accurately and fcientifically, *varieties,* not worth enumerating. Two of thefe however fhould be remembered, *viz.*

Allegoria — *inverfio, permutatio:* a continued metaphor: *parturiunt montes nafcitur ridiculus mus.* The entire heathen mythology was by all the Greeks and Romans, except the vulgar, confidered as allegorical. An *allegory* differs from a *fimile* in this: in the former the fubject proceeds without interruption; in the latter, you ftop the fubject, for the purpofe of comparing it with fomething fimilar.

Hyperbole — *fuperlatio,* is lying without deceiving: thus: *nive candidior* — *minus nihilo* — *teftudine tardior* — ftrong as an elephant — fwift as an arrow — beautiful as an angel, &c,

Hitherto,

Hitherto, you know, we have been fpeaking of what are called *Tropes*, which Rhetoricians diftinguifhed from *Figures:* by thefe they underftood the mode of improving or adorning common language, not only by an artful application of *words*, but of entire fentences. Thefe figures are fo numerous, frequently fo infignificant, fo puerile, and fo confounded with their *Tropes*, that they are not worth remembering.

I fhall finifh my long epiftle with what I conceive to be the beft method of acquiring that moft defirable of all human accomplifhments, proper, graceful, and perfuafive elocution. I fay *the moft defirable*, becaufe the moft brilliant, and effectual, whether our purfuit be power or emolument; and I dwell upon this affertion, becaufe it is impoffible to infpire a young mind with that degree of enthufiafm neceffary to the attainment of a difficult object, if he be not previoufly convinced of its importance.

Young men who are intended for the pulpit, erroneoufly imagine, that if they can read a chapter in the Bible without ftumbling, they are fufficiently qualified for the priefthood: " they learnt to read Englifh before they were fent to a grammar-fchool;

from

from that time, therefore, it was ufelefs to attend to what they had already learnt."— Hence it comes to pafs, that fo many of our Clergy read a chapter in the Bible no better than a Charity-boy.

The requifites in a good reader or a good fpeaker, are diftinct articulation, proper pronunciation, proper emphafis, melody and pitch of voice, energy, animation, graceful attitude and action. Now, though Nature may have beftowed fome of thefe requifites on a few favoured individuals, yet thefe individuals are thinly diftributed; but we have the fatisfaction to know, that, with due attention and affiduity, thefe requifites may certainly be acquired.

Diftinct articulation is to be acquired by frequently reading aloud and flowly; at firft, very flowly.

Proper pronunciation depends principally on a critical attention to the proper found of all the vowels in our language. I know a Clergyman, who has defervedly the reputation of a good preacher, whofe preaching, neverthelefs, is, to a nice ear, extremely difgufting; becaufe, from a provincial habit, in his pronunciation he mif-fpells almoft every word he utters; his *a* is an *e*, his *e* is

an

an *i*, his *o* is a *u*. Surely a very little attention would have corrected this constant impropriety.

Proper emphasis will depend principally on a perfect comprehension of your author's design, and on a clear discrimination of the words which he meant to be emphatically expressed: without this discrimination, you will constantly pervert his meaning, and the finest compositions will lose their effect. The best means of acquiring the habit, the art, of emphatic expression, is to read aloud, repeatedly and slowly, the orations of Demosthenes and Cicero, in the original Greek and Latin; to study them inquisitely as you proceed; to translate parts of them into your native language; to read that translation to your associates, and to mark the effect.

Melody and pitch of voice. A sweet toned voice is, doubtless, a very valuable gift from Nature; but, in its natural state, it is *vox et præterea nihil.* It is a fine *Stradevarius* in the hands of a *Crowdero.* The organs which produce the human voice, form a musical instrument, made by that Divine hand, whose works no art can rival. Nature also gave us diamonds; but she left them for Art to polish. By constantly playing upon a

musical

mufical inftrument, we not only improve its tone, but we gradually acquire that degree of dexterity which is neceffary to give it a complete effect. So it is with the human voice. You muft practife with the unremitting affiduity of a young mufician, until you have familiarized every poffible modulation.

Energy in fpeaking, like the mercury in the barometer, fhould rife and fall with the weight of your fubject; and your proper ufe of this power will depend on your clearly underftanding the comparative importance of its feveral parts.

Animation will always be in a direct *ratio* of your own feelings. Like two mufical ftrings in perfect unifon, your own heart muft vibrate, before thofe of your audience can feel.

Graceful attitude and action, may feem to be the work of Nature. It is evidently a miftake. Nature may give fine features and limbs fafhioned in her beft mould, to a clown; but, whoever beheld a clown ftanding in a graceful attitude, or raife his arm like *Veftris?* It is evident that gracefulnefs in reading, in fpeaking, and in acting, is incompatible with the leaft degree of em

I

barraff-

barraffment. If an Orator be not perfectly at eafe, he will give to his audience rather pain than pleafure: they perceive his embarraffment, and they feel it: let it, therefore, be his firft care, to diveft himfelf of that troublefome companion which the French call *mauvaife honte*; that offspring of confcious inferiority; that badge of low breeding; that frequent, very frequent, obftacle in the road to pre-eminence; that difgrace of man!

But, you will afk me, by what means this gracefulnefs, this urbanity of manner, is to be attained? Is it by precepts or rules?— By neither; but by example and by practice: for, without example, you can form no idea of a *je ne fcai quoi*; a thing incapable of defcription. Yet, in faying, that it is to be learnt by example, I do not mean that the *manner* of any individual orator is to be copied. No: he muft be ftudied folely for the purpofe of affifting your mind in forming a juft idea of that kind of action and attitude, which, at once, diftinguifhes a man of the polite world from a ruftic.

Where are we to look for thefe examples, thefe modals of gracefulnefs?— In the Senate?— I have heard, in my time, fome

graceful

graceful fpeakers in either houfe — moft in the houfe of Lords; but many more in both, who would have difgraced a debating fociety in the City. Shall we then feek thefe mo- dels at the Bar? — I fear, at the Bar, there is not much *grace* to be found: yet there are, who both fpeak and *act* like gentlemen. The pulpit? — Alas! the orators from the pulpit, have, in this kingdom, long fince, refigned *action*, the moft powerful inftrument of Rhetoric, to St. Crifpin and his difciples. The Stage, then, is our *derniere refort*; and a miferable refort it is! There are not, in general, a more — I will not fay *gracelefs* — you would call it a pun; but, I will fay, a more *aukward* fraternity of *gentlemen*, any where to be found. If, however, you wifh to form a juft idea of all the beauty arifing from attitude and from motion, (particu- larly of the arms,) of which the human body is capable, you will fee it — not to imitate — in the perfon of an Opera Dancer.

Hamlet's inftruction to a fet of ftrolling players, will illuftrate what I have written.

" Speak the fpeech, I pray you, as I pro- nounced it to you, trippingly on the tongue: but if you mouth it, as many of our Players do, I had as lieve the Town-cryer had fpoke

my

my lines. And do not faw the air too much
with your hand thus, but ufe all gently; for
in the very torrent, tempeſt, and, as I may
fay, whirl-wind of your paſſion, you muſt
acquire and beget a temperance that may
give it ſmoothnefs. Oh, it offends me to
the foul, to hear a robuſtous periwig-pated
fellow tear a paſſion to tatters, or very rags,
to ſplit the ears of the groundlings, who,
for the moſt part, are capable of nothing
but inexplicable dumb ſhews and noife. I
could have ſuch fellows whipt for overdo-
ing termagant: it out-herods Herod. Pray
you avoid it."

Vale.

LETTER XV.

AMBITION is a virtue or a vice as its object is juft or unjuft. In Alexander *qui æftuat infelix angufto limite mundi*; in Cæfar, in Lewis XIV. the object of their battles was power and dominion, to which they had no juft claim: the firft and laft trampled on the univerfal law of nations; Cæfar broke the facred laws of civil compact. But the ambition to excel in poetry, in mufic, in painting, in mathematics; or to command an army, a fleet, or even to govern the ftate, is a virtue; not becaufe it may raife an individual, but becaufe the emulation of many individuals muft eventually benefit the community. In abfolute monarchies, fubjects rife to power more frequently on the wings of vice, than of virtue; of intreague, than of abilities. In ariftocratical or democratical governments, ambitious, cunning, refolute men, without probity or abilities, often rule the ftate. Why?—Becaufe a republic is a body without a head: it wants that fupreme executive

I 3   power,

power, which can annihiliate a dangerous minifter by a frown.

In the mixed government under which you have the felicity to be born, as the Minifter is refponfible for the mifconduct of the King, fo is the King, in fome degree, anfwerable for the mal-adminiftration of the man whom *he delighteth to honour:* and this implied refponfibility is juft; becaufe the conftitution gives to the King the power of chufing his fervants. Some of our Kings, either for want of penetration, or in confequence of perfonal attachment, have been very unfortunate in the choice of their Prime Minifters; but the confequences of their mifconftruing individual men, were fo fatal to themfelves, that future Kings of England will be cautious whom they truft.

In our prefent firft Minifter we have a fine example of what power and dignity may be attained by fuperior underftanding, in conjunction with application and good morals. Without thefe in an eminent degree, his being the fon of the late Lord Chatham would have availed him nothing. That good morals fhould have been a ftep to Mr. Pitt's elevation, would to the politicians

cians of the Machiavelian fchool, have appeared ridiculous; but I will venture to affirm, that, if Mr. Pitt, be his abilities what they may, had been a gambler, or had been known to debafe human nature by any fpecies of debauchery, we fhould never have beheld him in his prefent exaltation. Lord North, by a feries of unfuccefsful attempts to prevent the independence of our American brethren, had loft the confidence of the nation, and, by an enormous accumulation of the national debt, had ruined our credit both at home and abroad. So fituated, no human policy or power, without an immediate reftoration of that credit, could have faved us from abfolute perdition.

Now, to produce this great, this important effect, it was neceffary to chufe a firft Minifter eminently confpicuous for abilities, application, knowledge, refolution and integrity. It feems very extraordinary that thefe five effentials fhould have been generally perceived and acknowledged in fo young a man.

The firft of thefe *abilities*, that is, a capacity to learn, is doubtlefs a boon from Nature: in this boon, however, fhe is more generally liberal than Indolence is willing to allow.

allow. The remaining four effentials, every young man of abilities may poffefs; otherwife the want of them were unjuftly reprehenfible.

I have before obferved, that Mr. Pitt's moral character was the *primum mobile* of his elevation; and I found this obfervation on the recollection of there being, at the time of his appointment to the Miniftry, feveral members in both houfes, of diftinguifhed abilities; but, in the then critical fituation of this country; when our falvation depended on an univerfal confidence in the integrity of the Minifter; it was wifely determined, that a young man of at leaft equal abilities, but of irreproachable character, was moft likely to retrieve and re-eftablifh that credit and confidence fo neceffary to our exiftence.

Britain, at the conclufion of the American war, refembled a fhip, heavily loaded; her rigging and timbers fhattered in the late ftorm; her crew fatigued and difpirited; her officers either unfkilful, or worfe; a dangerous navigation; no land in fight, and without a pilate. Defpair marked the countenance of every man on the Quarter Deck. What was to be done?—" Pleafe

your

your honour, fays the Boatfwain to the
Captain, we have a young Midfhipman on
board, who underftands navigation as well
as any man in the King's fervice; he's always at his books and charts, and never
neglects taking an obfervation at noon. If
your honour will make him Pilate for the
voyage, I am fure God will fave the *Bri-
tannia*; for this young man neither gets
drunk, nor gambles, nor fwears an oath."

The ftrongeft argument in favour of virtue, is, that vicious men have no dependence on vice; and that, in every diftrefsful
emergency, they fly to virtue for protection.
Let us imagine a fhip, in the fituation of
that in the firft fcene of Shakefpear's *Tem-
peft*. Sailors believe that fhipwreck diffolves
all fubordination. Neverthelefs, fuppofe
them now caft on an unknown coaft; every
individual fufpicious of his companions;
apprehenfive of favage men and beafts, and
confcious of the neceffity of appointing a
commander. Their quondam Captain is a
man of abilities; but they have no opinion
of his honefty; they knew him to be a gambler, and inattentive to the duties of religion. The firft Lieutenant, on the contrary,
is a man of equal abilities, of ftrict morals,

and

and approved integrity. Can there be a doubt on whom the choice would fall? Every failor, how profligate foever, is convinced, that, in the deftribution of the wreck, a dif- honeft Captain will appropriate to his own ufe the beft part of the fpoil, and he ve- rily believes, that Providence will hear the prayers and profper the exertions of a good man.

Mr. Pitt's elevation may be confidered, not only as the means of refcuing this na- tion from impending ruin; but as a fine . example to young gentlemen, ftudents at our Univerfities, who, from family or for- tune, may expect a feat in Parliament; where hiftorical information, uniformity of cha- racter, and natural or acquired elocution, muft, in defpite of every obftacle, lift them into the higheft employments in the ftate, What a glorious incentive to application!

I have faid elocution *natural* or *acquired*; becaufe I have no doubt, that elocution, this moft defirable and moft beneficial of all qua- lities, though fometimes a natural endow- ment may be always acquired. If we may credit the Grecian hiftorians, Demofthenes, the prince of orators, had originally, in fpeaking, an indiftinct articulation; a na-

tural

tural ftammer, an impediment in his fpeech: they tell us, that, in order to cure himfelf of this defect, he practifed fpeaking with pebbles in his mouth, probably on the fame principle that a man walks in boots the day before he intends to run a race.

Be this anecdote true or fabulous, we may, I think, rationally conclude, that Demofthenes, finding in himfelf every requifite to become a diftinguifhed orator, except diftinct articulation; animated by that noble enthufiafm which is the foundation of great diftinctions in fociety, refolutely determined, by unremitting affiduity, to attain, by art, that which nature had not beftowed. He knew the ineftimable value of perfuafive elocution in a government like that of Athens: he knew the power of an orator, who, as Virgil elegantly fays — *regit dictis animos et pectora mulcet* —

Ovid, too, though perfectly fenfible of the power of beauty, afcribes the paffion of the Marine deities for the hero of the Odyffey, entirely to his elocution.

Non formofus erat, fed erat facundus Ullyffes,
Et tamen æquoreas torfit amore Deas.

Having thus wandered into claffical recollections,

collections, it is impoffible to forget the following elegant panegyric on elocution, of
the Roman orator — *Neque vero mihi quidquam præftabilius videtur, quam poffe dicendo
tenere hominum cætus, mentes allicere, volunta-
tes impellere quo velit; unde autem velit, dedu-
cere.*

If then it be true, that Eloquence is the
moft infallible ftep-ladder to fame, power
and emolument, how fhall we account for
its being totally negle&ted, as a branch of
education, in both our Univerfities? What
are the probable advantages of mathematical learning, or, from a critical knowledge
of Greek and Latin poetry, compared with
what might be expe&ted from a regular
courfe of le&tures on Eloquence, delivered
by the Public Orator, or by a profeffor of
Oratory? There are profeffors of Arabic and
profeffors of Mufic; but we look, in vain,
in the red book, for a profeffor of the only
art or fcience, call it which you pleafe, by
means of which young men can expe&t to
diftinguifh themfelves in the fenate, at the
bar, or in the pulpit.

· There are in this, and probably in every
other Univerfity, many ftudents who know
themfelves, in point of fortune, totally independent

dependent of the world, and confequently carelefs of its future fmiles or frowns; but I am perfuaded, that, if the utility of the fyftem of education were more apparent, they would apply. *Damn it*, fays a Fellow Commoner, *what have I to do with Mathematics? and as for Homer and Virgil, I learnt enough of them at fchool.*

I humbly conceive, that Quintilian fhould be particularly recommended to every ftudent in the Univerfity; that it would be a proper text for a courfe of lectures, and that every pupil, of a certain ftanding, fhould be repeatedly exercifed in public declamation.

The prefent Prime Minifter may poffibly, in fome future period, find leifure to beftow a little confideration on a matter of fo much importance as the reformation of the Univerfities. He was himfelf educated at Cambridge; he cannot therefore be infenfible of the Gothic abfurdity of a fyftem, which is not well calculated for the education either of Gentlemen, Lawyers, Phyficians, or Divines. Neverthelefs, I am very far from intending the moft diftant reflection on any individual in the Univerfity. The imperfections are not recent abufes; but the natural refult of an

un-

unavoidable adherence to the ſtatutes of eſtabliſhments which do honour to this na-tion, and which have, incontrovertibly, been of infinite benefit to mankind.

I am, &c.

LETTER XVI.

YOU have, I think, frequently been present when the question, "Whether private or public education be most eligible," has been discussed by men of candour and abilities; and probably you recollect, that the principal arguments in favour of the latter are,—that, in public schools, boys become better classical scholars; that, mixing with a greater variety of characters, and, being, in a greater degree, left to themselves, they are better qualified to mix with the world at large. The chief argument in support of a more private education, is,—that in this line, a greater attention is paid to the religion and morals of the pupils, and therefore, those who have been more successful in private stations, are generally men who have been privately educated.

If these arguments be founded on truth, we may rationally suppose, that a young man issuing from a public school, comes to the University in a state of nature; with a mind unimpressed with any fixed principles of religion or morality, and consequently

under

under the abfolute dominion of ftrong paf-
fions, at an age when Reafon, their only
poffible counterpoize, has hardly begun to
dawn. At a more advanced age, when reafon has acquired fome ftrength, it may be
a fufficient defence againft the attacks of
vice; but, in its infant ftate, it has no power; therefore Religon is the fole guardian of
young men emerging from a public feminary.

On this confideration, the college of which
you have the honour to be a member, wifely
ordains, that your academical ftudies fhould
commence with a commentary on that book
which is the foundation of the religion you
profefs. " What (fome of your fellow ftudents will fay) have we to do with the Chriftian Religion? We are not all intended for
parfons; and if we were, it will be time
enough to ftudy divinity when we take Orders."— In anfwer to this foolifh rhapfody, I
repeat;—the College, confidering that young
men, from public fchools, come to the Univerfity mere claffical fcholars, totally deftitute of religious or moral inftruction, hath
wifely conceived that the evident morality
of the Gofpel would be the moft immediate and effectual counterpoize to vice, until
reafon,

reafon, independent of religion, fhould acquire fufficient ftrength to convince them,
that vice is the extreme of folly.

In your convivial affociation with your
fellow-frefhmen, you will frequently hear
the early and conftant attendance at Chapel,
exclaimed againft as a *bore*. Neverthelefs,
there are arguments of confiderable weight
in favour of this inftitution. Early rifing
is certainly conducive to health; not only
becaufe the morning air is falutary, but becaufe it muft neceffarily induce an early re-
tirement to reft. Thofe who rife late read
little, and their laft hours of the day, or rather night, are often fpent in a manner dif-
graceful to human nature, and irrecoverably
deftructive to body and mind.—*Tenebras
magis quam lucem amaverint homines, quippe
quorum prava forent opera.*

Young men that keep good hours are
rarely immoral. There is yet another argument in favour of early devotion, which
a young mind capable of religious fenfibi-
lity, will feel: I mean the fatisfaction of having began the day in a manner moft ac-
ceptable to his Creator. This reflection will
infpire him with confidence; it will raife his
fpirits; it will make him fatisfied with him-

K   felf;

felf; it will confequently banifh all propenfity to ill temper, and render him a pleafant
companion to all his acquaintance. I never
meet with a peevifh, ill-tempered fellow,
without fufpecting that all is not right within. I cannot help fuppofing that he has
reafon to be diffatisfied with himfelf; becaufe a long acquaintance with human nature, in various climates and fituations, hath
convinced me, that chearfulnefs and good
temper are the natural produce of inno-
cence.

But thefe falutary effects of early devotion
neceffarily fuppofe a mind fufceptible of reflection; a mind capable of perceiving the
hourly dependence of the creature on its
Creator; a mind naturally difpofed to believe the truth of the Chriftian religion on
the credit of the wifeft men that ever exift-
ed in any age or country. Locke and Newton were both zealous Chriftians. With
regard to their fincerity *there is not a loop to
bang a doubt on*, and furely no human beings
were ever better qualified to feparate truth
from falfehood.

I do not mean to infinuate, that, in the
important article of Religion, it were wife
finally to reft your faith on the opinions of
other

other men: in mentioning Locke and Newton, I have no other intention than to prove
the reasonableness of relying on their judgment, until time shall have ripened your
own, and until you may have leisure to
read the best authors that have written in
support of divine Revelation.

- I cannot close this grave epistle without
advising you to contract no intimacy with
young men whose parents or guardians, by
supplying them with large sums of money,
lead them into perpetual temptation to frivolous and vicious indulgences. By exhaust-
ing your credit, you may possibly keep pace
with them for a time; but, the moment you
are aground, they will laugh at your distress,
and, without giving you any assistance, will
pursue their voyage, damning your stupi-
dity for pretending to sail with *them*.

One would not imagine that hunting and
horse-racing could be an admissible part of
University education. The vicinity of Newmarket, and its frequent meetings, now constantly attended by the first personages in
the kingdom, are doubtless irresistible temptations to young gentlemen who are not
sent to the University in pursuit of knowledge; but alas! the example is inevitable

 de-

deftruction to thofe ftudents, who, without the means, are feduced to imitate their fuperiors in rank and fortune; to thofe ftudents who were fent to the Univerfity for the only rational purpofe for which Univerfities were originally inftituted.

I do not prefume to arraign the conduct of royal perfonages. Horfe-racing, unconnected with gambling, may be an innocent amufement; but, having always conceived that money is the fole object of wagers, I cannot imagine why perfons who can never want money, fhould become gamefters. But, allowing that young princes find fome amufement in throwing handfuls of counters—to princes, guineas are mere counters—upon the turf, for blacklegs to fcramble for, the confequences to princes are imperceptible; whether they win or lofe, they can never be diftreffed. Not fo with thofe who are feduced by illuftrious example.

Mantua, væ mifere nimium vicina Cremonæ!

Cambridge is indeed unfortunately too near Newmarket: not becaufe it is the fcene of perpetual horfe-racing; but becaufe it is the centre of illegal gambling of every denomination; the vortex of the moft difho-
neft

neft and moft contemptible members of fociety. That young men of family and fortune fhould condefcend to mix with fuch
mifcreants, for the paltry purpofe of win-
ning a few guineas, is fo glaring a reflection on the character of a gentleman, that
nothing fhort of ocular demonftration could
render it credible.

You have, I believe, heard me fay, that
I think mankind not only the leaft amiable,
but the moft irrational part of the creation.
The celebrated Dean of St. Patricks has
been frequently abufed for this opinion.
Let thofe who think otherwife compare the
horfes at Newmarket with the *men*. Let
them firft obferve them on the courfe. Let
them follow the Horfes into the ftable, and
the Men to that *Pandæmonium* in which gentlemen fpend the evening at Newmarket.
E O-tables—hazard-tables—card-tables—
Lords, Commoners, Fellow-commoners,
Penfioners, Black-legs, Highwaymen and
Pickpockets; lying, curfing, fwearing, cheat-
ing, blafpheming!—Can you poffibly contemplate fuch a picture without horror? I
hope you cannot.

Let us now fuppofe that a choir of An-
gels were to look down upon Newmarket,

(this

(this being their firſt view of the inhabitants of this planet,) and that they were aſked, whether, if they were obliged to ſojourn a while upon Earth, they would be men or horſes? is there a Spirit among them who would not prefer the latter mode of exiſt-ence?

It has been frequently obſerved, and I think juſtly, that individuals generally act more rationally than aggregate bodies of men: how ſhall we otherwiſe account for that legiſlatorial ſupineneſs which continues to poſtpone the total ſuppreſſion of theſe licenſed ſeminaries of vice; when there is hardly an individual in the kingdom who is not perfectly convinced, that all race-grounds, and particulaly Newmarket, are the nurſeries of ſharpers, the ſchools of highwaymen, and the graves of morality?

Human underſtanding is a plant, which, individually, advances very ſlowly to matu-rity; but its progreſs in ſociety is yet much leſs rapid. Many of the philoſophers of an-cient times ſaw, and deſpiſed, the abſurdi-ties of the heathen ſyſtem of religion, whilſt their reſpective nations continued their ado-ration of fictitious, immoral, profligate dei-ties. Probably the period is not very far

remote,

remote, when the Britifh Legiflature will comprehend, that the moft effectual means of annihilating that opprobrious race of highwaymen, fharpers and gamblers, were to ftrangle the Hercules in the cradle. The total abolition of Horfe-racing and Cock-fighting, would do more towards the prevention of thofe felonies with which this nation is peculiarly ftigmatized, than all the penal laws that can poffibly be invented.

Adieu.

LETTER XVII.

I RECOLLECT, that, in some part of my last letter, I gave you what seemed to me a sufficient reason why *Beausobre's Commentary on the Gospel of St. Matthew* was among the first books put into your hands by your Tutor. The College perfectly acquainted with your total ignorance of any system of Morality, and equally uninstructed in the fundamental proofs and tenets of Christianity; consequently, considering you as a vessel launched into a dangerous ocean without a compass — wisely begins your University education with the institutes of Christianity.

To you, who have been told that the late King of Prussia was a declared infidel in regard to the divine origin of Christianity, it must appear strange, that the above mentioned Commentary should have been undertaken at the command of that monarch. The translator's preface tells you, that — It having been represented to his Majesty that the French versions of the holy Scriptures, being, by length of time, become obsolete

and

and unintelligible, it was neceffary to make a new tranflation, he ordered Meffrs. Beaufobre and Lenfant to undertake the work; which they executed, with the addition of a commentary on all the difficult paffages, &c.

This attention to the Gofpel in the Pruffian monarch was not the effect of his religious veneration for the writings of the Evangelifts; it muft therefore be afcribed to his political fagacity: it was, however, an evident acknowledgment of its importance to fociety, and a plain confeffion of its neceffity. But, be his faith what it might, in his various correfpondence with Unbelievers, he always fpeaks of the morality of the Gofpel with veneration.

A human Being totally deftitute of religion, is not a degree above the brute creation. Particular fyftems of Religion out of the queftion, it requires very little reflection to perceive, that the wonderful creation around you is not the effect of any fortuitous arrangement of inanimate matter; an opinion, though ftrenuoufly maintained by fome philofophers, much too abfurd to deferve a ferious refutation: It is fuppofing an *effect* without a *caufe*, than which nothing can be more ridiculous. What were the

fenti-

fentiments of the inimitable Cicero on this
fubject?

*Quid poteft effe tam apertum, tanque perfpi-
cuum, cum cælum fufpeximus, cælefiaque con-
templati fumus, quam effe aliquod Numen præf-
tantiſſimæ mentis quo hæc regantur?*

Mr. Addifon in his celebrated trajedy,
makes his hero, in confequence of a fimilar
reflection, exclaim

———— If there's a pow'r above us,
(And that there is, all nature cries aloud
Through all her works) he muft delight in virtue:
And that which he delights in, muft be happy.

This is doubtlefs a rational conclufion.
But the reafoning faculties, which diftinguifh men from brutes, were not beftowed
for the fole purpofe of contemplating the
creation, but to guide us through the in-
tricate paths of life. Man, I had almoft
faid *unhappily*, unendowed with *inftinct*, that
unerring reafon of Nature, received from
Heaven the power of ratiocination, of recollecting and comparing his ideas; of forming conclufions, and confequently of diftin-
guifhing good from evil. Hence, the conftitution of Virtue and of Vice. Without
this power of difcrimination, Virtue could

have

have had no exiſtence, and Vice was as neceſſarily the conſequence of the exiſtence of
Virtue, as vallies are produced by the elevation of mountains, or darkneſs by the ab-
ſence of light.

On this philoſophy is founded the Chriſtian doctrine of rewards and puniſhments:
a doctrine ſo rational and ſo juſt, that it
burſt prophetically on the imagination of
the almoſt inſpired Cicero. Scipio, relating
his dream, tells his auditors, that, meeting
his father, Paulus Emelius, in the cœleſtial
regions, he ſaid, among other things,—*juſ-
titiam cole et pietatem, quæ cum magna fit in
parentibus et propinquis, tum in patria maxima
eſt: ea vita via eſt in cœlum, et in hunc cætum
eorum, qui jam vixerunt, et corpore laxati,
illum incolunt locum quem vides.*

As to the ſouls of thoſe *qui ſe corporis vo-
luptatibus dediderunt*, he excludes them heaven, until, as a puniſhment for their crimes,
they have ſpent ages in fluttering round the
Earth, *circum Terram ipſam volutantur.*

Horace too, you remember, in his charming Ode to Mercury, aſcribes to him the
grateful office of conducting pious ſouls to
heaven.

Tu

Tu pius lætis animas reponis
Sedibus ——

So that, you see, the most distinguished literati, in an age when human genius seems to have reached its *ne plus ultra*, were powerfully impressed with a belief of future existence and of reward and punishment. They saw the unequal distribution of good and evil on Earth. They were convinced of the power and benevolence of the Creator. It was impossible to suppose him an unjust Being: therefore they were under the necessity of concluding, that virtue must be rewarded in another life.

But, we are told, that Virtue is its own reward. So it is, to a certain degree. In equal situations the virtuous man will be incomparably the most happy; but this does not secure him from the gripe of penury, from the heart-rending pangs of a Lear, inflicted by *a thankless child!* No, these are sufferings which no virtue could support, without the soothing expectation of a happier eternity.

That virtue is its own reward in our intercourse with mankind, is most true. Vicious men are mistrusted and despised, even

by

by the vicious themfelves. A man without character foon becomes an outcaft of fociety. Let it therefore be your firft care to eftablifh a firm character for fcrupulous veracity. A lie admits of no apology. This truth is fo generally underftood, that even among the moft profligate, what is called *giving the lie* muft be atoned for at the hazard of life. But, do not therefore haftily conclude, that you are to fend a challenge to every ill-mannered or drunken puppy who dares to difpute your veracity. I mean only to prove the vice of lying to be fo univerfally detefted, that to tell a gentleman he is guilty of it, is the moft unpardonable offence; and very juftly, becaufe it is, by implication, calling him a coward. A man of true courage will difdain the protection of a falfehood, were it even to fave his life. When he has once paffed the *Rubicon*, he will march boldly on to the capital. He has *put his life upon a caft*, and will nobly *ftand the hazard of the die*.

There is indeed, in this *trait* of a great character, no medium; and it becomes infinitely defirable when you reflect on the influence it will have on all your actions. If you are pofitively determined to preferve

your

your veracity, you will feldom perpetrate
what you would be afhamed to confefs. Be
Truth therefore your *Palladium:* I cannot
bequeath you a better inheritance.

Vale.

LETTER XVIII.

I SHALL in this letter resume the subject of personal Courage, which Mr. Addison, some where, calls *active fortitude:* it is a subject of too much importance to a young man to be lightly dismissed. I remember when, in the year 1778, I was waiting at Portsmouth to embark for America, I became acquainted with the Mr. Walters, who sailed round the world with Lord Anson, as chaplain to the Centurion, and who published the account of that voyage. He was an intelligent man, a rational divine, a generous host, and a pleasant companion.

One morning, as we were walking together on the rampart, and casually speaking of *fear*, he emphatically said, *Fear! fye upon it! it is an ignoble passion, and beneath the dignity of man!* — I could have hugged him to my soul; yet there was nothing strikingly new in this sentiment. Probably I had heard it many times before; but never so emphatically expressed, nor so perfectly in unison with my own feelings at the time. The impression on my mind became indelible.

There

There is fomething fo irrefiftibly bewitch-
ing in perfonal courage, that we have hardly
an inftance of a truly brave General or Admiral, who was not adored by every foldier,
or failor, under his command. Shakefpeare,
who was no novice in the knowledge of human nature, makes the young and beautiful
Defdemona violently enamoured of a gallant
foldier, a Moor, and already

———— declined
Into the vale of years.

But, fays this amiable heroine,

I faw Othello's viffage in his mind,
And to his honours and his valliant parts
Did I my foul and fortunes confecrate.

Ariftotle, if I remember right, in his Ethics,
affigns to Courage the firft place in his enu-
meration of moral virtues; and with reafon; for there is nothing more precarious
than the virtue of a coward: he fhrinks at
the approach of danger or difficulty, and
yields to temptation, for want of refolution
to refift it. The beft proof of a man's real
Courage, is to dare, in every fituation, to
be juft to his own principles, to himfelf, to
his

his connexions, and to the world. Men so fortified may say, with Horace,

Si fractus illabatur orbis,
Impavidum ferient ruine.

And, let me tell you, be your future pro-spects through life ever so flattering, you will, most assuredly, be thrown into situa-tions, where you will be exceedingly glad to repose on your conscious integrity: you will most certainly find it, by far, your best sup-port under the various disappointments, calumny and ingratitude of a strange, a very strange world!

There are, I believe, few men, who, when they begin to throw off the boy, do not make some sort of resolution to establish a character in the world, and to act like men of honour; unfortunately, they meet with temptations which they did not expect, and they swerve under a *salvo*, that they wish to be honest, but that it is every man's duty to do the best he can for himself and family. This is a most egregious mistake. There is but one honesty, one honour, one inte-grity, one virtue. They are all either ab-solute, or they do not exist; and I appeal to those men who have thus swerved from

                    what

what they knew to be right, whether the recollection of their deviations from the plain path of virtue, does not now confti-tute their greateft infelicity?

I have mentioned *honour*; I will therefore give you my idea of a man of honour. Per-fonal courage is doubtlefs a neceffary part of his character; and this effential he fhould eftablifh at his firft emerging into man: not by a querulous propenfity to contradiction; not by a promptitude to take offence; but by that cool and fteady demeanour, which may convince his affociates of his refolution to maintain his own rights, and to fupport his friend in a juft caufe, even at the ex-pence of a little prudence. This part of his character once eftablifhed, he will run very little rifk of future infult.

About the middle of the prefent century, I was member of a club, in the country, the prefident of which, a worthy clergyman, generally drank milk-punch; and, thence, in derifion, it was called *the Milkfop Club.* One evening two of our members, a choleric Phyfician and a young Divine, were engag-ed in a violent difpute.——"Sarrah," fays the Doctor, "if it were not for that band of thine, I would foon teach thee better manners."

——The

——The young parfon, without fpeaking a word, deliberately took off his band, and laid it on the table. The Doctor's choler inftantly fubfided, and the company laughed heartily at this conclufion of the duel. Now, though this behaviour of the Divine might not be ftrictly canonical, yet it gained him more general efteem than the beft fermon he could have preached.

A *man of honour*, a *gentleman*, they are fynonimous terms, is eminently diftinguifhed from the reft of mankind, by the uniform unreftrained rectitude of his conduct. Other men are honeft in fear of the punifhments which the Law might inflict: they are religious in expectation of being rewarded, or in dread of the Devil, in the next world. A *gentleman* would be juft, if there were no written laws human or divine, except thofe that are written on his heart by the finger of his Creator. In every climate, under every fyftem of religion, he is the fame. He kneels before the univerfal throne of God, in gratitude for the bleffings he has received, and in humble folicitation for his future protection. He venerates the piety of good men of all religions. He defturbs not the religion of his country, becaufe the agita-

tion

tion of speculative opinions, produces greater evils than the errors it is intended to remove. He restrains his passions, because they cannot be indulged without injuring his neighbour or himself. He gives no offence, because he does not chuse to be offended. He contracts no debts which he is not certain that he can discharge, because he is honest upon principle. He never utters a falsehood, because it is cowardly, and infinitely beneath the dignity of a Gentleman. He bribes no man for his vote, because he will not make a villain. He measures all offences by the intention; but he resents with the spirit of a gentleman, every palpable insult; because, in the present humour of the world, it is the only means of preserving good manners, and of securing to himself that respect, which, as a just man and a gentleman, he deserves.

Adieu.

L E T-

LETTER XIX.

YOU have afked me a queftion, to which it is as difficult to give you a pofitive anfwer, as to any query that ever went to Delphi; and, in imitation of that wife Oracle, my opinion fhall be fuch, that it may become negative or affirmative, according to circumftances.

To learn, or not to learn, Mufic? that is the queftion. I have a great deal to fay upon this fubject; you muft therefore prepare yourfelf for a prolix epiftle. If you happen to be deeply engaged in ftudies of more importance, you may poftpone the perufal, till you have more leifure: there is nothing fo *fpiritual* in the matter as to caufe it to evaporate.

By *learning Mufic,* I fuppofe you mean learning to play upon fome mufical inftrument. This may feem a captious diftinction; but an habitual accuracy of expreffion will gradually induce precifion in thinking. There is indeed a very material difference between learning Mufic, that is, learning the Science of Mufic, and learning to play

 upon

upon an inftrument. The exercifes required of one who fits for the degree of Doctor
in Mufic, are compofitions, not manual performance; and there are many excellent
bands who are totally ignorant of Mufic.

I am particular, perhaps pedantic, upon
this fubject, becaufe it is that concerning
which people in general, (thofe who are not,
in fome degree, *initiated)* fpeak moft *illite-
rately,* if I may be allowed the expreffion.
Even the common words *harmony* and *melody*
are perpetually mifapplied by perfons who
know nothing of Mufic: nor is there, in
this, any juft caufe of furprife, when we
find that our beft Lexicographers were ignorant of the diftinction. That Coloffus in
literature, Dr. Johnfon, explains the word
Melody by *harmony* of found. It is of Greek
derivation; or rather it is a Greek word,
μελωδια, and when applied to Mufic could
never mean *harmony,* of which the Greeks
had no idea. *Harmony* (αρμονια, concord, from
αρω, *apto,*) is a word that cannot be properly applied to Mufic, but to exprefs the
effect of two, three, or four notes, or tones,
vibrating or founding at the fame time. *Melody,* on the contrary, expreffes an agreeable
fucceffion of fingle tones, fuch as may be

executed

executed by a voice or a flute, or by any other wind-inftrument. Stringed inftruments are capable of producing harmony, becaufe two or more notes may be ftruck at the fame inftant.

It is not uncommon, when young gentlemen or young ladies who have learnt to play a little, are ftanding behind a performer, to hear them fay — " O, that piece is in a *fharp*, or in a *flat* key " — judging from there being *flats*, or *fharps*, marked at the beginning of the movement. Now, it is an equal chance that they are wrong: it depends on circumftances, of which they are totally ignorant; but which are known by a muſician the moment he hears the firft *chord* ftruck by the inftruments. I fhall explain this hereafter.

But nothing is more ridiculous than to hear the audience at a Concert vociferate their applaufe, in a foreign language, of which they do not underftand a word. Whether the finger be male or female; whether it be *one* performer, *two* performers, or a *chorus*, they mean to applaud, the cry is always *bravo!* What muft an Italian female think of an Englifh audience, who thus

com-

compliment her, as if fhe were a man? or
when they thus exprefs their approbation
of a *duetto*, as if it were fung by an individual? I do not expect that every gentleman
or lady who is prefent at a Concert or an
Opera, fhould underftand Italian; but furely
it were prudent not to rifk the ufe of words
in public exclamation, until we know their
meaning.

Catches and *Glees* are much in vogue, and
are confequently frequent fubjects of converfation, yet there are few people, totally
ignorant of Mufic, who do not want to be
told, that they differ materially in their conftruction; that in a *Catch*, the three voices
take the parts alternately, fo that each voice
fings the whole in turn: but that in a *Glee*,
all the voices begin at the fame time and
fing different parts, from firft to laft.

Now, though all this may be confidered
as knowledge of little importance, yet it is
fo eafily acquired, and indeed fo neceffary
to thofe that mix with mufical people, that
no gentleman fhould be without it. This
fort of knowledge is fufficient for the ge-
nerality; but a man of fcience fhould know
more. He may be ignorant of Mufic as an
Art;

Art; but, as a Science, he ought not to be unacquainted with its foundation, its eſſence, its conſtitution.

All muſical ſounds, whether of bells, of organ-pipes, of flutes, harpſichords, violins, &c. are produced by vibrations in the parts of theſe inſtruments, excited by ſome external cauſe. Theſe vibrations cauſe ſimilar undulations in the air, which ſtriking on our organs of hearing, brings, from the inſtrument, that vibration which excites in us the idea of the tone produced. Theſe inviſible undulations in the air, have, not unaptly, been compared to the waves ſuddenly produced on a ſmooth body of water, by a ſtone thrown into it: theſe waves are ſeen to expand, in all directions, in concentric circles from the ſpot where the ſtone fell. Sound, in like manner, expands in every direction, and the extent of its progreſs is in proportion to the impulſe on the vibrating cord or bell.

Admitting this theory, if every identical tone excite a peculiar undulation in the air, how happens it, that the various undulations produced by a rapid ſucceſſion of tones, do not perplex and deſtroy each other?—— If you throw a ſtone into a fiſh-pond, and, imme-

immediately after, another, and then a third, if you look very attentively, you will perceive, that their refpective circles will proceed without interruption, and ftrike the fhore in regular fucceffion. This experiment may be more fatisfactorily made, on your table, in a large trough of Quickfilver. If you ftrike the furface at one end, with your finger, and then immediately at the other, you will fee the waves of each run to the oppofite extremity of the trough, paffing each other without producing any confufion or interruption. This by way of illuftration; but furely the fact is a fufficient demonftration, that the atmofphere poffeffes the faculty of conveying founds in the moft rapid fucceffion, or combination, as diftinctly as they were produced. It poffeffes the power not only of receiving and propagating fimple and compound vibrations in direct lines from the voice or inftrument; but of retaining and communicating founds with equal fidelity, after repeated reflections and reverberation, as you have often been convinced by the found of French-horns among the hills. I fhall purfue the fubject in my next letter: till then, farewel.

L E T-

LETTER XX.

HAVING, in my laſt letter, accounted for the production and propagation of muſical ſounds, the next natural queſtion is—What is the cauſe of *high* and *low*—or, to ſpeak more muſically, of *grave* and *acute* ſounds or tones? — Theſe depend on the quick or ſlow vibrations of the ſounding body; that is, on the greater or leſs number of vibrations, in a given time. Large inſtruments and long ſtrings, produce grave or deep tones; ſmall inſtruments and ſhort ſtrings, on the contrary, produce acute or high tones; in organ-pipes, for example, in proportion to their length and dimenſions: this is alſo true of muſical ſtrings. If I take a muſical ſtring of any length, and divide it into two equal parts by a bridge in the middle, each half ſounds an octave, (that is, eight notes) higher than the tone of the whole ſtring. Their vibrations, relative to the whole ſtring, are as 2 to 1: therefore, they perform the ſame number of vibrations in half the time; and conſequently the octave

tave coincides with the fundamental note only at every fecond vibration.

But you will now afk, how it happens, as thefe vibrations gradually ceafe, that the tone continues the fame, till it is heard no more? It were natural to fuppofe, as the acutenefs of the found depends on the celerity of the vibrations, that as they become flower towards their decline, the tone would grow deeper, or more grave. If it were true that they vibrate gradually flower, the objection would be unanfwerable. But the fact is otherwife. As a pendulum performs all its ofcillations in equal times; its greateft range in the fame time as its leaft; fo a mufical ftring makes its firft long vibration in the fame time as its laft fhort one; for this reafon, the tone is uniformly the fame from firft to laft.

In proof of what I have faid concerning the length of ftrings, you obferve, that the ftrings, of this harpfichord, which make the high notes are the fhorteft, and that they gradually increafe in length as you defcend to the deepeft note of the inftrument. Now though there be black and white keys on this harpfichord, and each of thefe ftrike a

dif-

different note, yet the real number of notes is no more than seven, which are called by the first seven letters of the alphabet. If you begin with A, and strike seven notes in succession upwards or downwards, you will, either way, come again to A: they are not indeed the same notes as that with which you began; but they are octaves to it, vibrating, the one in half, the other in double the time.

These seven notes are those of a peal of seven bells: when there are eight, the smallest bell is an octave to the largest. But if musical instruments contained no other than these seven notes and their octaves, they would produce no better melody than that wretched jumble of sounds called ringing changes; or, at best, but a very simple tune: therefore to render these instruments more comprehensive, intermediate notes, called semitones, were introduced, each half a tone higher than the note below it, and consequently half a tone lower than the note above. These are the short white keys on the harpsichord. In consequence of this arrangement, the whole octave consists of 12 semitones, for they are each half a tone higher or lower than the next.

But,

But, you will afk—if there be feven whole notes, and if there be a femitone between every two, why does not the fcale confift of 14 femitones?—This is a very natural queftion.

The reafon, why there are but five inter-mediate notes, is, that, in this natural fcale, there are two places which require none; the two notes, between which thefe inter-vals lie, being only half a tone afunder. Why it is fo, I know not; but, you may immediately convince yourfelf, that it is a law in Nature, which your ear compels you to obey. Sing eight fucceffive notes, from the loweft to the higheft, or the reverfe, like a peal of eight bells when they ring *round*, as they call it, and you will, without knowing it, make an interval of but half a tone in two different places, namely, between the 3d and 4th, and between the 7th and 8th notes of the fcale: thus 1—2—34—5—6—78. But thefe half-intervals are not ab-folutely confined to the places where you fee them in this example: the ear will bear them in the following pofition, 1—23—4—56—7—8. In this laft feries, you obferve, the half tones lie between the 2d and 3d; 5th and 6th. Now, if you dot thefe notes
with

with one finger on the harpſichord, beginning with A, and touch none of the ſhort
keys, you will find, after a few repetitions,
not only that the ear will bear it; but, that
there is a mildneſs, a ſwavity, in the effect
when contraſted with the firſt *modus*. I ſay
modus, for they are the ſame *diatonic* ſcale,
conſiſting of the ſame number of ſemitones.
It is called the Diatonic ſcale to diſtinguiſh
it from the Chromatic, which aſcends and
deſcends by half tones, and which being
artfully mixed with the other, produces the
various modulations in modern compoſiti-
ons. The ancients, we are told had other
ſcales, in which their tones were more minutely ſubdivided. Our ſcience of Muſic
requires no ſuch ſubtilties.

The firſt of theſe modes is the *ſharp*, or
major, the ſecond, the *flat*, or *minor* key; for
there are no more than two *keys*, or, more
properly, *modes*; and theſe, be the fundamental, or key-note, what it may, are always determined by the *third* being *flat* or
ſharp; or, in other words, by the interval of
half a tone lying between the ſecond and
third, or between the third and fourth note
of the ſcale. There is one thing more to
be obſerved of this *flat* key, namely, that if

you

you begin with C, the flat 3d, the femitones will occur in the fame order as in the firft *modus*. You will obferve that any of thefe notes or half-notes, on the harpfichord, may be made the fundamental or firft note of the fcale in either *modus*; which note gives name to the key in which you modulate, and with which you muft neceffarily conclude the piece: But whatfoever note you make the key-note, the femitone-intervals muft fall in their proper places; and this can be attended with no difficulty, as the inftrument confifts entirely of femitones. But, before we try the experiment, it is neceffary you fhould know, that every femitone takes, occafionally, either the name of the note above or of that below it: thus, this half note between G and A is G *fharp*, that is, half a tone higher than the natural G; or it is A *flat*, that is, half a tone lower than the natural A.

If now you begin with C, and proceed upwards, note by note, you find the femitone-intervals lie in their proper places, namely, between the 3d and 4th, and between the 7th and 8th, without the neceffity of introducing any of the fhort black keys. But if you now make D your fun-

damental

damental note, in order to make two femitones, according to the major key, between
the fecond and third note in the fcale, you
are under a neceffity of taking the F *fharp*;
and, when you come up to C, the fame neceffity recurs, becaufe there muft be a whole
tone between the 6th and the 7th, and but
half a tone between the 7th and the octave.
For thefe reafons, when a piece of Mufic is
compofed in D with a *major* third, there is a
double crofs prefixt on or between the lines
where F and C are pricked, fignifying that
thefe two notes are *fharp*. If on the contrary,
you make B *flat* your fundamental note, and
proceed upwards in the major key, you will
find yourfelf obliged in order to make the
femitones fall between the 3d and 4th and
7th and 8th as before, to take in E *flat:* fo
that B and E muft be marked flat at the beginning of the movement: neverthelefs, this
movement has a fharp third, and is confequently in the major key. But if, with the
fame fundamental note, you change the femitone-intervals, according to the minor
modus, then A, B, D, E and G, will be *flat*.
Flats are marked by a fmall *b*, as the fharps
are by a double crofs.

You hear Muficians talk of *Cliffs* and of

M

Time,

Time, *triple* and *common*. That their language may not be totally unintelligible to you, I will give you such information, as, I think, every gentleman, liberally educated, should possess.

Musical notes are written or engraved, on or between five fundamental lines, to which there are occasionally added one or two more in the writing or engraving. Now, in order to avoid the obvious inconveniency of adding too many of these occasional lines, *Cliffs* were invented, by which any particular line, or interval, may be made the place of any note in the scale: if, for example, I make the place of G the lowest line but one, as in the common *Triple Cliff*, then the note in the interval above will be A, and that in the interval below will be F, and so of the rest. But if I make the upper line but one, F, as in the *Bass Cliff*, then the interval above will be G, and the interval below will be E. There are other Cliffs to answer the same intention; but this is sufficient to explain the design and conveniency of this arbitrary method of fixing a particular note on any line or interval.

Many years ago, I had the pleasure of being acquainted with a Mr. Roebuck of

Heath,

Heath, near Wakefield in Yorkſhire, a gentleman of fortune and a *gentleman*-fidler:
by a *gentleman*-fidler, I mean a ſcraper; for
ſuch, gentlemen fidlers generally are. "Damn
it," he would ſay, " thoſe raſcally compoſers
invented theſe Cliffs on purpoſe to puzzle
gentlemen."—I do not, with Mr. Roebuck,
believe that they were invented with that
intention; for they are frequently of indiſ-
penſible neceſſity; but they are often introduced, particularly in the Muſic of the laſt
age, when there is not the leaſt occaſion
for them. The wanton introduction of various Cliffs is certainly wrong. I ſhall tell
you ſomething about *Time* in my next letter.

Adieu.

 L E T.

LETTER XXI.

TIME, abstractedly confidered, inde-
pendant of visible motion, is less difficult to conceive than to explain or define.
The Aristotelians made sad nonsense of their
definition of Time—*numerus motus secundum
prius et posterius*. But though we cannot
easily explain our idea of absolute Time,
what we mean by relative Time, may be
communicated with great facility. The annual and diurnal motions of the Earth are
performed in certain fixed portions of absolute Time: these portions therefore may
be divided and subdivided into months,
weeks, days, hours, minutes and seconds;
which seconds are distinctly marked by the
swing of a pendulum of a certain length.
Some attempts have been made to apply
these regular oscillations of pendulums to
musical Time, so as to determine the absolute duration or length of each note. It
was an idle project, because it were useless
and impracticable.

Musical Time is merely relative, and must
always be arbitrary. It depends on the
fluc-

fluctuating tafte of the age, and on the executive powers of the performer. In the modern ftyle of performance, a *prefto* movement muft be played with the rapidity of lightning.

There are, in Mufic, but two kinds of Time. One is called *Common*, the other *Triple* Time. In the firft, when the notes in a bar are of equal length, the number is even; in the fecond, it is odd. By a *Bar* is underftood the fpace between any two of thofe perpendicular lines drawn acrofs the five lines ruled upon the paper. Let us fuppofe the following figures to be notes. 1234, 1234, 1234, &c. Now, if you fing thefe four figures to any tune you pleafe, and beat with your hand or foot whenever you come to the 1, you will fing in common time. If now you change your melody to *three* figures, thus—123, 123, 123, and beat as before, you fing in triple Time. A few repetitions of this very fimple practice, will, in five minutes, teach you that which many young ladies do not comprehend, after feven years inftruction. The fault is in the Mafter.

As to the length, continuance, duration, or protraction of each fpecies of notes, the fcholar is unnecessarily perplexed by a number

ber

ber of unmeaning names, such as *breves*, *semibreves*, *crotchets*, *quavers*, *semiquavers*, &c. It were much more rational, becaufe more intelligible, to call the fimple open circle, a *note*; when it has a tail, a *half-note*; when the head is filled, a *quarter-note*; when the tails are once tyed, an *eighth*; twice, a *fixteenth*, &c. Thus the name would exprefs the relative proportion of every note, and any farther explanation would be unnecef-fary.

So much for Scale, Mode, Key, Cliff, and Time. I told you, in a former letter, that modern Mufic differs effentially from that of the ancients, in the invention of *Harmony*, of which they appear to have been totally ignorant. I alfo told you that Harmony is the effect of two or more tones founding at the fame time. You will now afk, what is this Harmony?—and which are the tones that produce the effect?

Mufical Harmony has its foundation in a law of Nature: or, in other language, in a certain property inherent in peculiar modifications of matter: it depends on a coincidence in the vibrations of the founding bodies. No two ftrings vibrate in equal times, unlefs they be turned in exact unifon,

as

as are the two wires on a harpfichord, which form each individual note. I fpeak of a harpfichord without octaves. Unifon therefore is the only perfect concord. Other chords are more or lefs perfect as their vibrations coincide more or lefs frequently.

The next chord in degree of Harmony is the Octave, becaufe, as it vibrates in *half*, or in *double*, the time, the tones coincide at every fecond vibration. The Octave, you remember, is the tone of a ftring half the length: that is, the tone on each fide of the bridge, of a ftring divided into two equal parts. Now, if I remove the bridge, fo as to leave three parts of the whole ftring on one fide, and two on the other, the longeft divifion will found a 5th to the whole ftring, and if they were founded together, there would be a perfect coincidence at every third vibration: the 5th therefore is the next chord in rank.——You now move the bridge, fo that there fhall be three fourths on one fide; this longer part will found a fourth to the whole ftring, and their vibrations will unite at every fourth return. You then move the bridge fo as to leave four 5ths on one fide: the longeft divifion will found a major third to the open ftring, and the vibrations of

two

two ftrings in this proportion, will coincide at every 5th repetition. — And fo of other concords. Difcords are the tones whofe vibrations never coincide. They are neverthelefs of indifpenfible ufe in Mufic as a foil, and as the means of introducing concords with advantage.

In writing all this, I have not the moft diftant intention to make a Compofer of you. It is the philofophical part only of Mufic, which I have endeavoured to explain; that part which every philofopher (I fuppofe you intend to be a philofopher) fhould know, and which may be perfectly underftood without being able to play a note on any inftrument.

I mean now to confider your queftion — " Whether I would advife you to learn to play, and on what inftrument? " — From the following reflections you will collect my opinion of this matter.

The practice of Mufic, is, doubtlefs, an innocent and delightful amufement; and, becaufe it is delightful, very improper for thofe who have no time to fpare. But, fay the advocates for Mufic, it is a better relaxation and relief from ftudy, than mere idlenefs. There are two anfwers to this plea: firft,

firft, ftudious men require, in their relaxa-
tions, air and exercife — Mufic affords neither: fecondly, it has often happened, that
this relief which was at firft admitted as a
handmaid to Study, became her miftrefs:
nay, the baggage has fometimes been fo in-
folent as to turn her miftrefs out of doors.

When I firft began to fcrape on the violin, I was told, by my mafter, that unlefs I
determined to practife eight hours every
day, it was in vain to begin: yet people
learn Mufic for amufement; an amufement
that is conftantly to occupy a third part of
their whole time. There is indeed no art
that requires more conftant labour, if you
have the ambition to excel; to excel, I mean,
as a *gentleman performer*; for you will never
advance higher than a humble *Repiano* in a
good band. Now, whether the profpect of
arriving at this degree of excellence, deferve
the facrifice of one third of your time, admits of fome doubt.

If we reflect, that, from the beginning of
this century to the prefent time, many thoufands of men, in this kingdom, have been
labouring inceffantly to attain the art of
playing on the Violin, fome for amufement

and

and, others in their *vocation*; and that we have not yet produced one firft-rate player; is there not reafon to conclude, either, that it is infinitely the moft difficult of all arts, or that there is fome *fecret*, induftrioufly concealed from Englifhmen. Probably there is no fecret in the cafe; but there is a very unaccountable want of obfervation and re-flection, vifible in the *execution* of almoft all our violin-players.

When a boy firft begins to fcrape his gamut on the fiddle, he naturally makes every note by the motion of his whole right arm from the fhoulder. After he has prac-tifed for fome time, he acquires, from ne-ceffity, a little motion in the elbow, and with this he refts perfectly fatisfied. The proper motion of his wrift, if he underftood it ever fo well, would be incompetent to the execution of quick paffages, becaufe he plays with that part of his bow which lies be-tween the centre and the farther extremity; confequently when the notes are to be played on different ftrings, the arch defcribed by the right hand, extends beyond the power of the wrift; therefore the motion muft ne-ceffarily begin at the elbow, if not higher.

As

As this is a mechanical operation, if the propofition be true, it may be mathematically demonftrated: thus —

The part of the bow, in contact with the ftring of the violin, is the centre of a circle, of which the hair of the bow, from that centre to the extremity of the little finger on the right hand, is the *radius*; confequently this little finger moves in the circumference of a circle, which is greater or lefs, according to the length of that *radius*; and, as the length of the arch to be defcribed, in the fame time, depends on the magnitude of the circle, it is evident that an artift who executes difficult quick paffages with the part of the fiddle-ftick neareft his hand, will, *ceteris paribus*, execute thofe paffages with the greateft eafe. Let us fuppofe the bow to be divided into four equal parts: the hand of the artift who plays quick paffages on the firft, diftant divifion, defcribes, we will fuppofe, 20 archs of his circle, or plays twenty *quarter-notes* on different ftrings in a fecond of time: if he played with the centre on the fecond divifion of his bow, he would execute 20 *eighths*, and on the third, 20 *fixteenths*, in the fame time. But this is not the only advantage of playing near the hand: it brings

the

the execution within the range of the wrift, without any affiftance from the arm.

There is yet another effential difference between a common player and a capital artift: it lies in expreffion; which the firft endeavours to produce by the occafional preffure of his whole hand and arm; whilft, in the latter, it is entirely the effect of the fingers, not of the *left*, but of the *right* hand. His expreffive ideas do not ftop at his elbow, nor yet at his wrift: they pafs immediately to his fingers, like the feelings of a fine per-former on the *Piano-forte*.

. If now you obferve, with attention, Cra-mer's manner, and compare it with that of the fidlers about him, you will eafily con-ceive it impoffible for thefe gentlemen ever to pafs the line of mediocrity. But this perfect and indifpenfible knowledge of the principles of the art, is not, of itfelf, fuffi-cient to produce a capital performer on the violin. Nature muft previoufly have fa-voured the individual with a genius or ta-lent for Mufic; with an ear exquifitely formed, and capable of the moft minute difcrimination of founds.

Inftruments on which principal parts are played in Concerts, and which confequently

require

require rapid execution, muſt be begun with at a very early age, and the practice continued with a degree of aſſiduity, juſtifiable only in a profeſſed Muſician. But if you have a tolerable ear, are fond of harmony, and wiſh to be able to take a ſimple part in a private Concert, the Tenor-fiddle, the Violoncello, or the Baſſoon, may be learnt in a ſhort time, and retained by very moderate practice. If your ambition ſoar no higher than a Scotch ballad, the German flute is your inſtrument. By all means, avoid the Hautboy, out of compaſſion for your neighbours; unleſs, at any time, you want to drive the rats and mice from your apartment. As to the Harpſichord — I once ſat playing upon that inſtrument, in a room next the ſquare where I then lived. As two gentlemen were paſſing the window, I heard one of them exclaim, — "I hate to ſee *a man* at the Harpſichord!" I had never before annexed the idea of effeminacy to that inſtrument; but from that moment, I began to be of the gentleman's opinion.

I think, the moſt deſirable muſical accompliſhment, is, the art of ſinging at ſight; that is, the art of hitting, or ſounding the notes with your voice as with an inſtrument.

ment. Poffeffed of this art, with a proper comprehenfion of time, you are, without being a profeffed finger, enabled to join in a Catch or Glee, which, of all Mufic, is the moft generally pleafing.

But, this art is commonly thought difficult to learn. I believe the difficulty originates in the abfurd method of teaching. If you have voice and ear fufficiently true to run the octave up and down, both in the major and minor key, you may, by the following fimple means, learn to fing at fight in lefs than a fortnight; provided you have, previoufly, a fufficient knowledge of *triple* and *common* Time, and of the relative length of the notes and refts: a knowledge that may be acquired in an hour.

For the letters of the alphabet, by which the feven notes are named, I fubftitute the feven firft figures, 1, 2, 3, &c. becaufe they will apply to any part of the harpfichord: begin where you pleafe, 1 is the fundamental, or key-note, 2 the fecond, 3 the third, and fo on to the octave.

Firft, run the feven notes, in the major key, from one octave to the other, backward and forward, till you can found them truly and eafily. Then practife the fame in the

minor

minor key, and, if you be not perfectly fure of the truth of your ear, touch the notes on the harpfichord as often as you are in doubt.

Having thus made fure of the notes in their natural order, in both modes, you may now proceed to ring changes on them thus. 1, 3, 5, 7; 7, 5, 3, 1.—then 1, 4, 6, 8; 8, 6, 4, 1: continuing to alternate thefe chords till you have them quite perfect. You may now take them in the following order: 1, 2; 1, 3; 1, 4; 1, 5; 1, 6; 1, 7; 1, 8;—then, 8, 7; 8, 6; 8, 5; 8, 4; 8, 3; 8, 2; 8, 1. When you are quite perfect in this third leffon, both major and minor, your fourth leffon may be in this progreffion—1, 3; 2, 4; 3, 5; 4, 6; 5, 7; 6, 8: then 8, 6; 7, 5; 6, 4; 5, 3; 4, 2; 3, 1. Prefuming that you can fing thefe four leffons with great eafe and certainty, you may proceed to the chromatic fcale, rifing by half-notes from the lower to the upper octave, and defcending in the fame manner; and now the great bufinefs is over. Take a fong, or any book of Mufic; pitch your key, and you will find, that, with a little practice, you will be able to hit the notes as certainly as with an inftrument.

It was a very juft obfervation of my worthy acquaintance Dr. J—— who is himfelf

a good

a good Muſician and an excellent ſinger, that ſinging has this great advantage over inſtruments, the learner may practiſe whenever he is alone, walking or riding; ſo that there is no loſs of time; whilſt one of the ſtrongeſt objections to the practice of inſtrumental Muſic is, that it requires more time than a ſtudious young man can ſpare.

Vale.

LETTER XXII.

A MIND, naturally inquifitive, one would imagine, muft feel diffatisfied in a ftate of total ignorance, relative to the furface of this terreftrial globe. The greateft number of mankind know nothing more of the planet they inhabit, than the town or parifh in which they were born. A fchool-boy, from a public feminary, is as ignorant of Geography as a peafant, and the fyftem of education at the Univerfities is not calculated to inculcate Geographical information.

There are, I believe, very few young gentlemen, who do not feel depreffed by this load of geographical ignorance. Every Newfpaper is an *opprobrium*. They read the names of towns and countries without knowing in what quarter of the world they are to be found; and they are afraid to afk queftions, which, they know, fome children could anfwer. They have feen Geographical Grammars; but thefe are fuch thick clofe-printed volumes, and feem to contain fuch a multifarious accumulation of fcience

and

and technical language, that they poftpone the ftudy of Geography, till they have at leaft fix months to fpare. Probably you will be furprifed when I aver, that all the Geography neceffary to a gentleman and a polite fcholar, may be taught in the compafs of a very few pages; perhaps within the limits of a moderate letter, or two.

What is the fcience of Geography? Its derivation from γη *terra* and γραφω *fcribo*, anfwers the queftion. It is then, a defcription of the Earth; a knowledge of the abfolute and relative fituations of empires, kingdoms, provinces, &c. It is generally made to include, *the ufe of the globes*, but improperly. Confidering the Earth as a globe, making a part of the folar fyftem, it becomes an objeft of Aftronomy. Geography is no farther concerned in the Earth's motion, and dependence on other bodies, than as they affeft the various climates on its furface. This fcience therefore may be ftudied with equal propriety, and much more conveniency, in the maps which cover the walls of this room, than on a terreftrial globe.

Let us begin with that in the centre: the map of the World. It confifts, you perceive,

of

of two large circles, which reprefent the two hemifpheres of the globe, fuppofing it cut into two equal parts. The broad external circles which furround thefe two hemifpheres reprefent the horizon; that is, the imaginary circular line, which, if you were raifed fo far above the Earth as to fee one half of it, would divide the vifible from the invifible half.

That ftraight horizontal line which divides the northern from the fouthern hemifphere, is called the *Equator:* on the Earth it is an imaginary, and, on a globe, a real circle. The double circle which paffes over the middle of New Holland, and that which you fee at the fame diftance from the Equator on the north fide, are called the *Tropics.* The other two double circles near the north and fouth poles, are the *Polar Circles.* They are of ufe in Geography in determining what are called the Zones. The fpace between the two Tropics is the *torrid*; between thofe and the polar circles, the *temperate,* and within thofe circles, the *frigid* Zones.

In this, and in all other maps, the top is the *north*; the bottom, the *fouth*; your right hand, the *eaft*; and your left, the *weft.*

Thofe circles, which you fee meet in both

 poles,

poles, are called *Meridians*. They paſs through every tenth degree of the Equator, and ſerve to mark the longitude: they are imaginary circles which would be formed by a line drawn upon the Earth over the ſpot to which the ſun is vertical at every tenth degree. The curve lines which are drawn from every tenth degree on the Horizon, ſerve to mark the latitude. By *latitude* is meant the diſtance from the Equator north and ſouth. *Longitude* is the diſtance, eaſt or weſt, from any particular Meridian: in our maps, it is generally taken from that of the Obſervatory at Greenwich.

You know, our firſt great diviſion of the Earth is into what are called four quarters: Europe, Aſia, Africa and America. Theſe we will ſucceſſively contemplate. But before we take our leave of this general map of the World, it is neceſſary that you ſhould particularly notice the ſituation of theſe four quarters relative to each other. The northern hemiſphere, you ſee, is occupied by Europe, Aſia, the greateſt part of Africa, and North America. In the ſouthern, we find no land except South America, part of Africa, New Holland, and a conſiderable number of iſlands in the Pacific Ocean.

Our

Our conftant intercourfe with the Eaft Indies renders an acquaintance with the fituation of that country indifpenfibly neceffary. You read of fhips making their outward or homeward voyage in fix, feven, eight months, &c.; they touched at the Cape of Good Hope; they watered at St. Helena. Now, is it conceivable that a young gentleman poffeffed of any curiofity, or the leaft inclination to knowledge, can reft fatisfied in the total ignorance of the diftance and fituation of places which affront him in every news-paper. The Cape is the fouth extremity of Africa, and the fmall ifland of St. Helena, you will find, in about fix degrees of weft longitude and fifteen of fouth latitude. Other remarkable places are New Holland, on the fouth-eaft coaft of which you will find Botany Bay, &c. and on the weft coaft of North America, in latitude 50, you will lay your finger on *Nootka Sound*, the prefent bone of contention between us and Spain. Before you quit this map, you will alfo take notice that the fea between Europe and North America, is called the *Atlantic*; that between America and the eaftern coaft of Afia, the *Pacific Ocean*; and

that

that which occupies the greateſt part of the ſouthern hemiſphere, the *South Seas.*

Having thus diſpatched the world in general, let us now contemplate this map of Europe; which, you perceive, is the Europe we have already ſeen, magnified, or delineated on a larger ſcale. Here the degrees of *latitude* marked on the ſides, and of longitude at the bottom, are much larger. By this means Europe becomes as large as the whole world; and, as theſe degrees may be enlarged to any ſize, a kingdom may be magnified to appear as large as this Europe, or a province as large as a kingdom.

Before we inveſtigate this quarter of the world, it is neceſſary to obſerve by what countries and ſeas it is environed. On the *eaſt* you ſee it is bounded by Aſia; on the *weſt*, by the Atlantic; on the *north*, by the Frozen Sea; and on the *ſouth*, by the Mediterranean. This ſea, you obſerve, is a principal object: it deſerves your attentive conſideration. It waſhes the coaſt of Spain, of France, of Italy, and of European Turkey. It contains the iſlands of Ivica, Majorca, Minorca, Corſica, Sardinia, Sicily, Candia and Cyprus, beſides the ſmall iſlands of the Archipelago,

chipelago, and others in the gulph of Venice. If you apply your compasses to that scale of English miles, and then stride them from one end to the other of the Mediterranean sea, you will find it about 2000 miles in length. With your compasses thus fixed, you can instantly measure any of the kingdoms, or states, in this map, or the distance between any two places.

The map being coloured, you immediately perceive the size and situation of the several kingdoms, &c. You observe the prodigious extent of the Russian Empire, and the remainder you will find covers an equal proportion of Asia. Sweden, though not very powerful, is next in size. France, Spain, Germany, Poland, Denmark and Norway, Turkey, England and Ireland, Italy and its appendages, differ not materially in dimensions. The small States and Kingdoms are, Holland, Switzerland, Portugal and Prussia; but you are not to estimate the territories of his Prussian Majesty, by the size of his *kingdom*. He is, besides, Elector of Brandenburgh in Germany, where you will find his capital, Berlin. To these the great Frederick added Silesia, which he took from the Empress, and obtained a considerable slice

of

of Poland, in a late partition between the two Empreſſes and himſelf.

You may ſometimes, in converſation, wiſh to recollect the latitde of the principal cities in Europe. The beſt method of fixing this in your memory, is to trace, with your finger thoſe that lie in, or near, the ſame parallel, thus: Beginning with the latitude 41, on the weſt ſide of the map, and paſſing a little above the line 40, you will firſt touch upon Oporto in Portugal; thence, travelling eaſtward, you will paſs through Madrid the capital of Spain; thence, over the iſland of Sardinia, to Naples in Italy: and thence to Conſtantinople. Theſe cities therefore lie in, or very near, the ſame degree of latitude, and therefore enjoy the ſame climate, except what differences may ariſe from local cir-cumſtances.

If now you move your finger up to 48, and proceed eaſtward, as before, you will paſs through Paris, Manheim, Ratiſbon, near Vienna, Preſbourg, through the upper part of Hungary and the ſouthern extre-mity of Ruſſia. About the latitude 52 you will find London, Amſterdam, Brunſwick, Berlin, Warſaw. In 56, paſſing from weſt to eaſt, on the ſame parallel, you will travel

through

through Edinburgh to Copenhagen, and thence to Mofcow. Peterfburgh, the capital of the Ruffian Empire, lies in 60, the latitude of the Shetland iflands.

In this map of Europe it is neceffary farther to remark, that, befides the Mediterranean, there are two other inland feas, viz. the Baltic and the Black Sea. The firft, you obferve, communicates with the German Ocean through the Categate, and the other with the Mediterranean, by the Archipelago. On the coaft of the Baltic there are feveral towns which deferve particular notice, as you find them frequently mentioned in the public accounts of the progrefs of the prefent war between Sweden and Ruffia. The ports on the Black Sea alfo merit your attention on account of the war between the Ruffians and the Turks. For the fame reafon you fhould mark the fituation of the principal towns on the borders of Turkey.

There remains nothing more, I think, of any importance, except the principal rivers, viz.—The Volga, which rifes in Mofcovy and falls into the Cafpian Sea at Aftrachan—The Don, whofe fource is not far from that of the Volga, but which runs to the Sea of Afoph — The Danube and the Rhine, both

which

which take their rife in or very near Switzerland.   The firft takes an eaftern courfe,
and, after paffing, as you fee, through Germany, Hungary, and Turkey, falls into the
Black Sea: the Rhine takes a contrary direction, runs through Germany and Holland, and difembogues itfelf in the German
Ocean.   Rivers of lefs note are the Elbe at
Hambourgh, the Tagus at Lifbon, the
Thames at London, and the Rhone in
France, which laft, you obferve, falls into
the Gulph of Lyons near Marfeilles.

As to our ifland, you fee it lies between
50 and 60 degrees of north latitude, that,
on the *eaft*, it is feparated from the Continent by the German Ocean; on the *weft*,
from Ireland, by St. George's Channel; and
on the *fouth*, from France, by the Englifh
Channel.

Vale.

LETTER XXIII.

WE now turn our attention to the map of Afia, in which, as in that of Europe, you fee, the Ruffian dominions cover the largeft fpace. In this vaft territory, there are few objects worth remembering, except Kamtfchatka, which is mentioned by fome of our northern navigators, and that inhofpitable region, called Siberia, to which Ruffian malefactors are banifhed. The firft of thefe lies between 55 and 60, the latitude of Scotland.

With Tartary we have no concern: with Arabia and Perfia, almoft as little. In Turkey, which is at the weftern extremity of the map, you find Smyrna and Aleppo at the eaft end of the Mediterranean. Thefe places are well known to our merchants trading to Turkey. You there alfo find Jerufalem and other towns mentioned in fcripture.

Thence we proceed to India, and tracing the coaft from Surat on the weft fide to the mouths of the Ganges at the eaftern extremity, you pafs in fucceffion, Bombay, Goa, and thence along the coafts of the Carnatic,

Mala-

Malabar, and Coromandel, till you come to Pondicherry, Madras, and so on to Calcutta. Hence, passing to the south of the Equator, we sail between the islands of Sumatra, and Java; leaving the Dutch settlement of Batavia on the right, we proceed directly north to Canton in China, and thence to Pekin at the northern extremity of that empire. All these are places with the names of which you have been long acquainted, and whose respective situations, I dare say, you will now remember. The several clusters of islands in this map, are those of Japan, of Sonda, the Philippins, the Ladrones, the Moluccas or Spice-islands and the Moldivias. That part of India with which we have any connection, lies, you observe, within the Tropic; that is, within 23 degrees and a half of the Equator: consequently the inhabitants have a vertical sun twice during their summer, and consequently the climate must be excessively hot. This, I think, is all that is necessary to be remembered of Asia; we therefore now change the scene.

Africa, you observe, forms a very considerable part of the habitable globe. It has hitherto been so imperfectly explored, that our knowledge extends but to a small diftance

tance from the coasts, in any part. On the *east*, it is bounded by the Indian Ocean; on the *west*, by the Atlantic; on the *north*, by the Mediterranean; and on the *north-east*, by the Red Sea. It extends from 73 degrees of north, to 35 of south, latitude; about 5000 English miles: consequently the Equator runs nearly through the middle of it.

If now you begin at the Straits of Gibraltar, here at the north-west corner of the map, and follow the south coast of the Mediterranean, you come first to Algier, then to Tunis, and then to Tripoli; which are the only places of any consequence on the coast of Barbary. Continuing your journey eastward, you arrive at Alexandria in Egypt, and passing the mouths of the Nile, you come to Grand Cairo; thence, travelling with the celebrated Bruce, between the Nile and the Red Sea, you traverse the kingdom of Nubia, and arrive in Abyssinia. From thence, still following the coast, you will not find a name that you have ever heard before, or that deserves to be remembered, till you come to the Cape of Good Hope, at the southern extremity of this continent. It is a Dutch settlement, in the country of

the

the Hottentots, a people with whom we begin to be better acquainted since the publication of some late travels into this part of
the world.

Having now doubled the Cape, you proceed northward till you come to the coast
of Guinea; thence you pass the rivers Gam-
bia, and Senegal on the Negro-coast, leaving, a little to the westward, first, the Cape
de Verd islands, then the Canaries, and finally the island of Madera. On the south
side of the Equator, you observe two small
islands, at a considerable distance from the
continent, St. Helena and Ascension, both
in the track of our East-India ships. . There
is also an island on the east coast of Africa,
called Madagascar, too large to have escaped
your notice.

This map of the continent of America,
and of the West India islands, requires to
be studied with some attention; particularly
North America, as without a competent
knowledge of that country, you cannot possibly understand the history of your own
times.

By North America is generally under-
stood that tract of country which lies between the northern extremity of Hudson's

Bay

Bay and the Gulph of Mexico. Between the latitude 55 and 50 you find, New South Wales and Labrador. This is a very cold climate, though in the same latitude with England. From 50 to 45, you have Canada, Nova Scotia, and Newfoundland. These are still very cold countries, though in the latitude of France. Between 45 and 40, lies New England. Thence you proceed southward through Jersey, Pensylvania, Maryland, Virginia, N. and S. Carolina, Georgia and Florida. Westward of these you observe Louisiana and the vast kingdom of Mexico, extending southward as far as Panama, within 7 degrees of the Equator.

From Panama down to Cape Horn, the south point of America, you pass no places of note, except Lima the capital of Peru, whence the Spaniards import Gold, and what is more intrinsically valuable, the *Cortex Peruvianus*. In latitude 33 you leave, a little to the west, the island of Joan Fernandes, rendered famous by Anson's Voyage. You now double the Cape, and passing Falkland's island, proceed northward along a desart coast till you come to Buenos Ayres at the mouth of the great river of Paraguay, which runs through an extensive country of

the

the same name; for an account of this river and country, I refer you to the *Travels* of my old acquaintance Don Antonio d'Uloa. About forty years ago, I had the pleasure of his company from London to Lisbon. He was a Philosopher, and lamented much that the Inquisition would not permit him to say, the Earth moves round the sun. You are now arrived at the Brasils, an extensive country, the coast of which is in possession of the Portugueze. Having doubled Cape St. Roque and passing the mouth of the vast river of the Amazons, you touch at the Dutch settlement of Surinam, and thence proceed along the coast till you come to Curasao, an island, also in possession of the Dutch. From this island they import that superior species of Tobacco which they call *Kanaster* or *Varinas*, the name of a town on the Spanish *Terra-firma*, in the neighbourhood of which it is cultivated by the inhabitants, who barter it with the Hollanders for European goods.

Hence we continue our coasting voyage till we arrive at Carthagena and Portobello, names that were familiar to every individual in Britain when I was a boy. We were then at war with Spain. Portobello

was

was taken by Admiral Vernon, who became the hero of the day, and the fign of an ale-houfe in every village. You now come to the Bays of Honduras and Campeachy, where we claim a right to cut Logwood, which right the Spaniards difpute whenever they want a pretence for quarrelling. Paffing Vera Cruz, you leave the city of Mexico on the left, and continue coafting the Gulph, till you come to New Orleans near the mouth of the famous river Miffiffippi, the project of a trade to which fomewhat more than half a century ago, about the time of our South Sea bubble, ruined half the people in France.

Your next objects are the iflands of Cuba and St. Domingo or Hifpaniola, as it is alfo called, belonging to Spain. Near the weft extremity of the former, you find the Ha-vanna, which the late Lord Albemarle and Sir George Pocock, took in the war preced-ing the laft. South of Cuba, lies our Ja-maica, and to the northward the Bahama iflands. Eaft of St. Domingo you fall in with another ftring of fmall ifles, the chief of which are Antigua, St. Kitts, Barbadoes and Nevis belonging to us; and to the

O

French,

French, Martinico, Guadaloupe, St. Lucia and Dominica.

Probably, before you quit America, you may wiſh to be more minutely acquainted with the ſcene of the late war with our rebellious children: a war by which they obtained their liberty: a war that coſt this nation much more money than would have purchaſed the whole country, and almoſt as many men as there are people in it: a war that has overturned the French monarchy, and kindled the torch of Diſcord in different parts of Europe: a war that in its conſequences has ſpread alarm among princes; but a war that immortalized four Engliſh Generals. The various ſcenes of their exploits you muſt look for at Boſton; on Long Iſland near New York; in the Jerſeys, particularly at Trenton; at Charleſtown, at Philadelphia, and at Saratoga.

There remains, I think, nothing more in this map of America, except this cluſter of iſlands, for the knowledge of which we are principally indebted to Captain Cook. I mean the Society Iſlands in the Pacific Ocean, between 15 and 20 degrees of ſouth latitude. In the centre of theſe you obſerve the celebrated Otaheitee.

Thus,

Thus, I flatter myfelf, I have fulfilled my promife, in communicating, in the compafs of two not very long letters, as much Geographical knowledge as you will ever want. In my next, I purpofe to fatisfy your curiofity relative to the four prints of *Pæftum* which I have lately hung up in my ftudy. Mean while,

I am, &c.

LET-

LETTER XXIV.

THAT you fhould recollect no claffical information concerning the city of Pœftum, is not very furprizing, as I believe that in the ancient authors you have read, there are but two paffages in which it occurs: one in the *Georgics*,

Forfitan et pinguis hortos quæ cura colendi
Ornaret, canerem, biferique rofaria Pæfti.

The other in the *Metamorphofes*,

Leucofiamque petit, tepidique rofaria Pæfti.

The original name of this city was Pofidonia, from Ποσειδων, *Neptunus*, to whom it was dedicated. When, and why, the Romans changed its name to Pœftum, I do not know. It is fituated in the gulph of Salermo, on the weftern coaft of Italy, about 60 miles fouth of Naples. Whether it was built by the Sybarites or by the Dorians, is matter of difpute; it is certainly however of very remote antiquity, if it be true, as the Sicilian Diodorus tells us, that Hercules in his travels refted on a rock in

the

the country of the Pofidonians. But, be
the original founders or poffeffors of this
city who they might, hiftorians tell us, that
whilft the Romans were yet in their infancy, Pofidonia was taken by the Lucanians,
a colony from the Samnites; that this people were difpoffeffed by the Romans, in the
year of Rome 480, at which time it became a
Roman colony, and afterwards a municipal
town.

About the year of Rome 528, when D.
Quintinus was fent againft Tarentum, we
learn, from Livy, that the three cities of
Rhegium, Velia and Pœftum furnifhed
twenty fhips to the affiftance of the Romans; the fame author alfo tells us, that,
fix years after, during the Punic war, Pœftum fent, by their embaffadors, a prefent of
golden cups, but that they were not accept-
ed. *— Legati a Pæfto pateras aureas Romam
attulerunt; iis, ficut Neapolitanis, gratia aɛ̃a,
non acceptum.* In another place, he makes
honourable mention of this city among
thofe, which, after the battle of Cannæ,
when the Romans were in great diftrefs,
generoufly affifted them with troops and
money, for which they received the public
thanks of the Senate and people.

                    From

From the time of the Roman Republic, till the ninth century of the Chriſtian *æra*, hiſtorians make no mention of this once magnificent city. But we learn that, in the year 866, Docibilis duke of Gæta, being at war with one of his neighbours the Lord of Capua, ſolicited the aid of the Saracens, a colony from Sicily, then eſtabliſhed in Calabria. They came to his aſſiſtance and remained in poſſeſſion of a conſiderable part of the country, whence they were finally expelled by means of a body of Greeks ſent by one of the Conſtantines. But, before their entire expulſion, in the year 930, they entered Pœſtum in the night, and after pillaging the inhabitants, ſet it on fire.

There remained yet conſiderable veſtiges of its ancient magnificence, till, in the year 1080, the pious zeal of Robart Guiſcard, ſtripped the ancient temples of their ornaments, for the purpoſe of adorning a church which he was then building at Salermo, where, he believed, the bones of St. Matthew were depoſited.

From the many Inſcriptions found in the ruins of this ancient city, I will ſelect the following, as one of the moſt remarkable,

TVLLI.

TVLLI. OLERII. POESTANI
QVI. VIX. Ā. LXXXXV.D.XI.
FF. XXVIII. NN. LXXXIII.
C. L. P.P.

I dare fay you will conftrue it without the leaft difficulty.

In the firft print, you have a profpect of the country, and of the ruins of Pœftum as it now appears at a diftance. Its walls, you fee, are wonderfully entire, confidering their great antiquity. The higher towers next the gates are fuppofed to be of more modern conftruction. Over the arch of the north gate, on the outfide, there is a figure of Neptune, carved on the key-ftone of the arch, and on that within, a *hippocampus*, or fea-horfe. The circumference of the city is about two miles and a half. It muft always have been an unwholefome place from its vicinity to the *Palus Lucaniæ*, and from the bituminous and fulphureous fprings with which it is furrounded: for this reafon the inhabitants were under the neceffity of procuring water from diftant hills, as appears by the ruins of feveral aquæducts.

The principal ruins within the walls are an Amphitheatre, a Theatre, and the three

Tem-

Temples which you fee in thefe three prints,
They are all what the Greeks called *amphi-
proftylos*, that is, having two porticos, one to
each front. The columns of thefe temples
are of the Doric Order, in its moft ancient
manner.

.Probably you will be furprized when I inform you, that the ruins of Pœftum were
firft difcovered about five and thirty years
ago. How this difcovery happened, I will
tell you, in the words of my worthy friend
Dr. Longfield, to whofe learned publication,
I refer you for a more circumftantial account of thefe ruins.

" In the year 1755, an apprentice to a
painter at Naples, who was on a vifit to
his friends at Capaccio, by accident took a
walk to the mountains which furround the
territory of Pœftum. The only habitation
he perceived, was the cottage of a farmer,
who cultivated the beft part of the ground,
and referved the reft for pafture. The ruins
of the ancient city made part of this view,
and particularly ftruck the eye of the young
painter; who, approaching nearer, faw, with
aftonifhment, walls, towers, gates, and temples. Upon his return to Capaccio, he con-
fulted the neighbouring people about the
origin

origin of thefe monuments of antiquity. He could only learn, that this part of the country had been uncultivated and abandoned during their memory; that, about ten years before, the farmer whofe habitation he had noticed, eftablifhed himfelf there; and that having dug in many places, and fearched among the ruins which lay round him, he had found treafures fufficient to enable him to purchafe the whole.

" At the painter's return to Naples, he informed his mafter of thofe particulars, whofe curiofity was fo greatly excited by the defcription, that he took a journey to the place, and made drawings of the principal views. Thefe were fhewn to the King of Naples, who ordered the ruins to be cleared, and Pœftum arofe from the obfcurity in which it had remained for upwards of feven hundred years, as little known to the neighbouring inhabitants as to travellers." Farewel.

LETTER XXV.

I MEANT, in some future letter, to have brought you acquainted with Botany in its proper place, as a branch of Natural History; but as the spring is the best season for beginning the study of this science, subjects of more importance must give place to it for a time.

Salvitur acris hyems gratâ vice Veris et Favoni.

Let us therefore turn our present attention to that beautiful part of creation

— *terræ quem ferunt solutæ.*

Botany was originally studied with an attention solely to the medical virtues of plants. The only ancient Greek author on this subject, whose writings are now extant, is *Theophrastus,* the disciple and successor of *Aristotle:* he flourished about 320 years prior to the Christian æra: he is said to have written ten books *On the history of Plants,* one of which is lost; and eight, *on their causes,* of which only six remain. In imitation of Aristotle's *Historia Animalium,* his book is

not

not a hiftory of particular plants, but of plants in general. He mentions about 500, but defcribes fo few with accuracy, and the reft fo very imperfectly, that fucceeding botanifts have been able to recognize but a fmall number of them. Probably Dr. Sibthorp, who has lately explored the country where Theophraftus herborized, may have afcertained many of his plants, and I hope he will not long withhold his difcoveries from the public. *Theophraftus* was firft tranflated into Latin by Geza.

The two later naturalifts worth notice, are Diofcorides and the elder Pliny; that unfortunate Pliny who perifhed in the fmoke of Vefuvius. They appear to have lived at the fame time, that is, about the middle of the firft century. Of the writings of Diofcorides only eight books have been preferved. He mentions about 600 plants; of thefe he defcribes about 400: but few of his defcriptions anfwer to our plants.

Pliny's work is entitled *de Hiftoria Mundi*, of which only 37 books are preferved. It is an indifcriminate collection of all that he had read of Natural hiftory. The vegetable part is a mere tranfcript from Theophraftus,

Diof-

Dioſcorides, and a few other writers whoſe works are loſt.

Pliny ſays, that Cato was the firſt Roman who wrote of Plants, and that, after him, one Pompeius *Lenæus*, a freedman of Pompy, tranſlated into Latin, *Notes and Obſervations* on Simples, written by Methridates, from papers taken by Pompy when he defeated that King. He alſo tells us that Evax, an Arabian King, wrote a book on the virtues of plants, a copy of which he ſent, as a preſent, to the Emperor Nero; that Cratevas, and others, publiſhed coloured drawings of plants; and that Antonius Caſtor, a Roman Phyſician, had a Bontanical Garden, in which he (Pliny) had ſeen moſt of the herbs he deſcribes. This Caſtor was then a hundred years old. Is it not a little extraordinary, that the name of Pompy's freedman, who tranſlated the papers of Methridates, ſhould ſo nearly reſemble that of *Linnæus*, the great author of our preſent ſyſtem of Botany?

If you have any inclination to know the botanical authors from Pliny down to our own Ray, you will find a ſhort account of each, and of their writings, in Tournefort's

Iſagoge

Ifagoge in Rem Herbariam. In this catalogue there is not a fingle writer, from the
firft to the fixteenth century, whofe botanical labours deferve the leaft attention.
Without methodical arrangement, natural
hiftory feems a chaos; yet no attempt at a
botanical fyftem appeared till the year 1583,
when Cæfalpinus, profeffor of Medicine at
Padua, publifhed his book *de Plantis,* in
which they were arranged according to their
fructification, or·manner of producing their
feed. But this fyftem laid dormant almoft
a century after his death, when it was re-
vived by Morifon, profeffor of Botany at
Oxford, in his *Hiftoria Plantarum, Oxonienfis,*
fol. 1680. To this fyftem fucceeded that
of our excellent botanift Ray, many years
a refident member of Trinity college, Cambridge. He formed his 31 claffes partly on
the diftinctions obfervable in the fhape of
the *corolla,* and partly on the fruit. He
publifhed his *Methodus Plantarum nova* in
1682; the firft volume of his *Hiftoria Plantarum* (which you may fee in the Univerfity
Library, in 3 huge folio volumes) was printed in 1686; and his *Synopfis ftirpium Britan-
nicarum,* in 1690. The beft edition of this
book is that publifhed by Dillenius in 1724.

The

The next fyftem was that of Tournefort, which he firft publifhed in French, in the year 1694, and in 1700, in Latin, under the title of *Inftitutiones Rei Herbariæ*, 3 vols. 4°. The 2d and 3d volumes confift entirely of plates, in all 475. He divides the vegetable kingdom into 22 claffes, characterized by the fhape and number of petals in the flower. His generic diftinctions are founded the fructification.

The firft of thefe three fyftems, invented by Cæfalpinus, was ill adapted to the inveftigation of ftrange plants, becaufe it was impoffible to difcover the clafs to which they belonged, till the feeds were completely formed. Ray's fyftem was, in part, liable to the fame objection. Tournefort's fyftem was natural and eafy enough, in the general claffification, and his *genera* are commonly afcertained with fufficient accuracy; but he goes no farther: fpecific characters made no part of his fyftem.

The Linnæan fyftem of Botany is now generally received and univerfally taught. It is confeffedly artificial; but much better adapted to the inveftigation of an unknown plant, than any of the former. His *Claffes* are fubdivided into *Orders*, and his *Genera*

into

into *Species* and *Varieties*. It is called the *Sexual fyftem*, becaufe he confiders the *Stamina* analogous to the male organs of generation in animals, and the *Piftilla* to the female. He divides the entire vegetable kingdom into 24 claffes, 23 of which are diftinguifhed by the number, or the comparative length, or the conne&ion, or the fituation of the. *Stamina*. The 24th clafs comprehends the plants in which the organs of generation are invifible. The *Orders* generally depend on the number of *Piftilla* in the flower: fometimes on other circumftances. The *Genera* are chara&erized by peculiarities in the flower; the *Species* by the leaves or ftem, and. the *Varieties* by accidental circumftances. ·

The firft thirteen *Claffes* and their *Orders*, are denominated from the number of *Stamina* and *Peftilla*; thus, *Monandria monogynia*, from μονος *unicus*, ανηρ *maritus*, and γυνη *mulier*: that is, one hufband and one wife, the flowers of this Clafs containing one *Stamen* and one *Piftillum*; and fo of the other thirteen Claffes and their refpe&ive Orders; for a circumftantial defcription of which, and of all the fucceeding Claffes, I refer you to your

your *Clavis*, which you will receive with this letter.

Probably you may have some curiosity to know who this celebrated Linnæus was; this inventor of the new system you are about to study. I will therefore give you a sketch of his life.

Charles Linnæus was the son of a Swedish Divine, and born in the year 1707, at Rœshult in the province of Smoland. He was, in his infancy, so attentive to the knowledge of plants, and consequently so negligent of his other studies, that his father determined to take him from school and to bind him apprentice to a shoe-maker. However, in 1717, he was sent to the University of Lund, and in 1728 removed to Upsala, where he persevered in his favourite study of Natural History, under the severe oppression of absolute poverty, until his singular abilities and application gained him the patronage of Olaus Celsius, professor of Divinity, and Olaus Rudbeck, professor of Medicine and Botany.

In 1731, he was sent on a botanical expedition into Lapland, and received, from the Royal Society of Upsala, the sum of

eight

eight pounds sterling, for his travelling ex-
pences. He was absent about a year and a
half, in which time he walked 4000 miles.
Soon after his return, he published his *Flora
Laponica*, in which the plants were arranged
and described according to his own new
syftem.

In the year 1735, he began his journey to
Holland, where, on the recommendation of
the great Boerhaave, he was patronized by
Mr. Clifford, whofe botanical garden he
fuperintended, and at whofe expence he
travelled to France and England. In 1738,
he returned to Stockholm, where he mar-
ried and fettled as a phyfician. In 1741, he
was appointed Profeffor of Botany at Up-
fala. In 1753, he was created *Knight of the
Polar Star*, and, three years after, enobled.
He died in 1778, aged 71.

The diftinction of male and famale plants
was, by no means, the invention of Linnæus.
It is as old as *Empedocles*, who wrote a book,
De natura et principiis Rerum, about the 75th
Olympiad, in which, as we learn of Ariftotle, he fpoke of plants as being oviparous,
and hermaphrodite. An Olympiad, you
know, was a period of 4 years, by which
the Greeks computed time: this *Empedocles*,

P

there-

therefore, muft have lived near a hundred years before Ariftotle, who was born about the 98th Olympiad. I dare fay you remember to have read, that this *Empedocles* threw himfelf headlong into Ætna, that the world might believe he was a God. He certainly convinced the world that he was a fool.

Ariftotle expreffes fome doubt of this new doctrine of vegetable generation, yet he tells us, that, if the duft of a branch from the male Palm-tree be fhook over the female, her fruit will foon ripen.

Theophraftus, the difciple of Ariftotle, obferves, that the chief diftinction among trees is their gender, male and female.

Diofcorides and Pliny, both fpeak of male and female plants, but without precife ideas of either. Cæfalpinus obferved the difference of fex in the Clafs of plants which Linnæus has fince called *Dioeciæ*. But *Zaluzianfki*, a native of Poland, who, I believe, wrote at the latter end of the 16th, or beginning of the 17th century, appears to have been the firft botanift who diftinguifhed the fexes of plants in their various modes of males, females, hermaphrodites, and *androgynæ*.

Many years after this, our countryman
Grew,

Grew, and other naturalifts of different nations, refumed the enquiry, and, by microfcopical obfervations, difcovered that the
females were impregnated by the *polen* contained in the *antheræ* of the males. On this
foundation Linnæus built his *Sexual Syftem*;
a fyftem entirely his own. We now return
to the other claffes.

Clafs XIV. DIDYNAMIA, has four *Stamina*,
two long and two fhort: the *Orders* are determined by the Seeds being naked or inclofed in a *Pericarpium*.

Clafs XV. TETRADYNAMIA, has fix *Stamina*, four long and two fhort. The *Orders*
depend on the form of the *Pericarpium*.

Clafs XVI. MONADELPHIA; *Stamina* united at the bafe; Orders diftinguifhed by the
number of *Piftilla*.

Clafs XVII. DIADELPHIA; *Stamina* generally in two divifions; the flower papilionaceous. The Orders fignified by the number of *Piftilla*.

Clafs XVIII. PALYADELPHIA; *Stamina*
in three or more divifions: Orders depend
on the number of *Piftilla*.

Clafs XIX. SYNGENESIA; Five *Stamina*,
united in the *Anthera*. Orders determined
by the formation of the *Flofculi*.

Clafs

Clafs XX. Gynandria; *Stamina* on the *Piftillum*. Orders diftinguifhed by the number of *Stamina*.

Clafs XXI. Monoecia; *Stamina* and *Piftilla* in feparate flowers on the fame plant. Orders, from the fituation or number of the *Stamina*; or from the uniting of their *Antheræ*.

Clafs XXII. Dioecia; *Stamina* and *Piftilla* on feparate plants. *Orders* the fame as in Clafs 21.

Clafs XXIII. Polygamia; *Stamina* without *Piftilla*, or vice verfa, or both together. Orders depend on the fituation of the *Stamina* and *Piftilla*.

Clafs XXIV. Cryptogamia; Parts of fructification not diftinguifhable. Orders, from habit or apparent refemblance.

You, who are a Greek fcholar, will find no difficulty in difcovering the etymology of the titles of thefe feveral claffes: You will then eafily fix them in your memory. But I fhall explain them farther in the examination of particular plants. This method of reading the great book of Nature, and of invefligating her productions in the order and fucceffion in which fhe prefents them to our view, I conceive to be far preferable to the dry method of learning Botany by

means

means of formal *Introductions* or *Rudiments,* the contents of which it is impoſſible to remember without examples, and which examples it is impoſſible to procure in ſtudying the ſeveral Claſſes in regular ſucceſſon.

I have no intention, in giving you this general introduction to the ſcience of Botany, to allure you from more important ſtudies. You are to regard it as a ſcience of amuſement; but, with this ſtrong recommendation, that it may be acquired without ſtealing a ſingle hour from your neceſſary lucubrations. We read of men, who, in the ſhort ſpace of human life, have acquired a degree of univerſal knowledge, to which one might imagine the age of an antediluvian would hardly have been ſufficient. The late illuſtrious Profeſſor Haller, of the Univerſity of Gottingen, was a remarkable example of this univerſality. He was a minute anatomiſt, an accurate phyſiologiſt, an indefatigable botaniſt, a charming poet, a claſſical ſcholar, an univerſal linguiſt, an aſtoniſhing bibliothecarian, and, in the latter part of his life, a moſt intelligent magiſtrate.

That a man of univerſal erudition was

no

no uncommon phenomenon among the ancients, appears from the following paſſage
in Cicero, who, in ſpeaking of the Greek
philoſopher, ſays — *in qua difficile eſt enume-
rare quot viri, quanta ſcientia, quantaque in
ſuis ſtudiis varietate et copia fuerint, qui non
una aliqua in re ſeperatim elaborarent, ſed omnia quæcunque eſſent, vel ſcientiæ perveſtiga-
tione, vel differendi ratione comprehenderent.*

Geſner, the great Swiſs naturaliſt, was ſo
aſtoniſhing a prodigy of knowledge, that
Boerhaave uſed to call him *Monſtrum erudi-
tionis.* His extenſive learning appears truly
wonderful, when we conſider, that he ſhone
in the midſt of a dark world; in an age of
groſs ignorance, and depreſſed by indigence.
He lived early in the 16th century.

Genius, application and memory, are
doubtleſs neceſſary to the attainment of
what may be called univerſal knowledge: by
univerſal knowledge, I mean an intimate acquaintance with ſome ſciences, and ſomewhat more than a ſuperficial knowledge of
the principles of all: but, I believe, the labour of becoming thus univerſally learned
is not ſo very herculean as we generally
imagine; and that it depends principally on

a jua judicious arrangement of our ſtudies, and diſpoſition of our time. In the arrangement of our ſtudies we ſhould imitate the ſkilful agriculturiſt, whoſe ſucceſſive crops ſo relieve each other, as to preclude the neceſſity of *fallowing*; and, as to the diſpoſition of our time, let us take Botany for an example. A man who ſtudies all day and every day, will, in a few years, become unhealthy and ſtupid: therefore, part of every ſtudent's time muſt be loſt in exerciſe. *Loſt* did I ſay? No: it is not loſt to a Botaniſt. He ſtudies where other men, for want of books, muſt lounge. To him the book of Nature lies conſtantly open. He reads as he walks along: every field is a new chapter; every leaf is an object of attention, and every flower a prize. A general knowledge of Botany therefore may be learnt at times when other ſtudies are neceſſarily ſuſpended; conſequently it interferes with no other ſcience. I ſay a *general knowledge*, which is enough for a gentleman who ſtudies Botany as an amuſement: an univerſal and minute botaniſt muſt unavoidably neglect things of more importance. In my next letter I ſhall lead you into the fields. — Remember to

take,

take, in one pocket, your *tin box*, and, in the other, the second volume of your *Synopsis**.

Adieu.

* *Synopsis of the Natural History of Great Britain and Ireland, printed for T. Cadell, 1789.*

LETTER XXVI.

MARCH, 1790.

IF you have read my laſt letter with attention, the 24 claſſes of Linnæus are
fixed in your memory: without a perfect
recollection of theſe, it is impoſſible to proceed a ſingle ſtep in the modern ſyſtem of
Botany. As to the *Orders*, it will be time
enough to look round the houſe when you
are introduced to the family.

Notwithſtanding the remarkable mild- *Bellis.*
neſs of the winter, you ſee, our botanical enquiries of to day, will be confined to a ſmall number of flowers.
The common Daiſy, and that yellow
ſtar, which you obſerved, in abundance,
on the declivity of the ditch near the
iron gates of King's, are the only flowers we have ſeen. Let us begin with
the moſt common of all flowers of the
field, the Daiſy, univerſally called, in
Latin, *Bellis*. The ſpecific, or trivial,
name, given by Linnæus to the ſpecies
in your hand, is *perennis*, to diſtinguiſh

it

it from the other, which he calls *annua*.
The firſt of theſe only, grows wild in
this kingdom. Notwithſtanding its
vulgarity, you will find it a very curious object. You will hardly believe
me when I tell you, that there are, in
that ſingle Daiſy, about one hundred
and twenty complete yellow flowers,
beſides fifty white ones without *Sta-*
mina.

As to its name, *Bellis*, ſays Ray, *Latinis*
a bello ſeu pulchro colore florum dicta creditur;
and its Engliſh etymology, we learn from
theſe lines of our ancient poet Chaucer,

> Well by reaſon men it calle maie
> The Däiſie, or elſe the Eye of the daie.
> And at the laſt there tho' began anon
> A Lady for to ſing right womanly
> A Bargonet in praiſing the Daiſie;
> For as methought among her notis ſwete
> She ſaid, *ſi douce eſt la Margarete.*

You will find this paſſage quoted at length
in Curtis's *Flora Londinenſis.*
If now you pull out one of the white external rays of this little flower, of which
there are about 58, by applying this mag-
nifying glaſs, you will find it tubular at

the

the bottom, and containing a single *pistil-lum*. You now detach some of the yellow florets which compose the disk; each of these you will discover to be a perfect tubular flower, containing 5 *stamina* and one *pistillum*. Now as each of these florets of the disk is provided with the male and female organs of generation necessary to the production of seed, the *pistillum* in the *radii* is superfluous; which circumstance determines the *Order* to which it belongs, viz. *Polygamia superflua*; and that it is of the Class *Syngenesia* is evident, because the flower consists of a number of florets comprised within one calyx, which is the general characteristic of that class. You are also to observe, that, in this class, the *stamina* are united at their extremities, so as to form a cylinder; and that, at the bottom of each floret, there is a single seed placed on the *receptaculum*. For the meaning of these and other technical terms, I must refer you to your *Clavis* *, where I have explained them according to what I conceive to be the Linnæan acceptation.

I need

---

* *Clavis Anglica Linguæ Botanicæ, or a Botanical Lexicon, &c.* the first edition of which I published when I was a student of Medicine at Edinburgh. It was originally written for my own use, and republished last year.

I need not tell you that the word *Synge-nesia* is derived from Συν, *simul*, and Γενεσις, *generatio*, and that it is the 19th class; a particular explanation of which you will also find in the book last mentioned.

Having now stript off all the florets, white and yellow, there remains, in your hand, a naked conical *receptaculum*; seeds without *pappus*; calyx hemispherical, composed of uniform scales; seeds obovate. These peculiarities determine the *genus*.

The Species is distinguished by the stalk being naked, *scapo nudo*.

If Chaucer, in the lines above quoted, alluded to this our common Daisy, probably he was mistaken in the French name, which is *Paquerete*. The plant which the French call *Margarite* is the *Chrysanthemum leucanthemum*, or Ox-eye Daisy; easily distinguished from the former by its size, the leaves on the stalk, &c.

From this specimen, I conceive, you have acquired botanical knowledge sufficient to distinguish the plants of the Class and Order, *Syngenesia*, *polygamia superflua*, wheresoever you may find them. Let us now examine one of those yellow star-like flowers which grow in such abundance in this field.

On

On the firſt infpeČtion, you per- *Ranun-*
ceive that the *ſtamina* are more than *culus.*
20; therefore it is of the Claſs *Poly-*
andria: and in the centre of the
flower, you find a great number of
germina, which are the female organs,
though without *ſtyli,* and their *ſtig-*
mata are very minute. This brings
it to the Order *Polygynia.*

As to the *genus* of this plant, authors differ. The celebrated Haller and Hudſon,
make it a diſtinČt genus, and call it *Ficaria*
verna. But our great maſter Linnæus muf-
ters it among the *Ranunculi,* and he is fol-
lowed by Curtis and Relhan. Theſe are in-
diſputable authorities. This is the generic
charaČter of the Ranunculus—*Calyx penta-*
phyllus; Petala quinque, intra ungues poro mel-
lifero. Now the flower in your hand has a
calyx of but 3 leaves, and the petals are 8
in number; but theſe differences which are
not invariable, are inſufficient to conſtitute
a new genus. The ſcale and *neČtarium* at
the baſe of each petal; their gloſs and the
general *habitus* of the plant declare it to be
a Ranunculus.

The Species we diſcover, by its leaves being heart-ſhaped, angulated, on long *petioli;*
and

and by each ftalk fupporting a fingle flower. This defcription agrees only with the *ficaria:* fo that we now no longer hefitate to call our plant the *Ranunculus ficaria* of Linnæus, or Pilewort; of which you will find a very good plate, well coloured, in my copy of the *Flora Londinenfis.*

Cal- tha. On the oppofite fide of that ditch, you fee a yellow flower, fomewhat larger than this, apparently of the Ranunculus *genus.* It is indeed of the fame Clafs and Order, viz. *Polyandria Polygynia,* but differs from the *Ranunculi* in having no *calyx,* no *nectarium,* and in its feeds being inclofed in capfules. It refembles the *Ranunculi* in having 5 rounded petals; but they are not glazed on the upper fide. The flowers grow in pairs on feparate *pedunculi.* The leaves are heart-fhaped. It is the *Caltha paluftris,* the only fpecies of that genus hitherto found in any part of the world. You will find them in almoft every fwamp, and particularly in very great abundance on the morafs at the back of Peter-houfe.

I fup-

I suppose Thomsom meant this Water-
lily in these lines,

——————— See how the lily drinks
The latent rill, scarce oozing thro' the grass,
Of growth luxuriant, or the humid bank
In fair profusion deeks.

Under those trees, in the language of the
same poet,

——————— where purple violets lurk
With all the lowly children of the shade,

you will find some purple flowers. You
know them to be violets by the smell. But
you wish to learn to what Class and Order
they belong. Carefully inspecting the centre of the flower, you will discover 5 stamina, the *antheræ* of which are united. Now
this being the essential characteristic of the
Syngenesia, it certainly is of that class; but,
as in this Violet, we do not find a number
of florets inclosed in one common calyx, it
must necessarily belong to the Order *Monogamia*; which differs remarkably from the
other 5 Orders of this class, in the flower
being simple. This Order excepted, the
class Syngenesia is perfectly natural. The
generic character of the Violet is, Calyx of
5 leaves;

5 leaves; Corolla of 5 petals, irregular, horned behind; Capfule above, trivalve, unilocular. The Species is determined by the plant producing no Stem; the leaves being heart-fhaped, and fuckers creeping. It is called by Linnæus *Viola odorata*. In the *Flora Londinenfis* you will fee the minute parts of the Violet with more eafe than in the natural flower.

Of the *genus* Viola, there are 28 fpecies; only 6 of which have been found in this kingdom, and but 4 in Cambridgefhire, as you learn from my friend Relhan's valuable *Flora*. Thefe are

Viola odorata, fufficiently diftinguifhed by its fmell.

V. berta, is inoderous and hairy; the *bracteæ* grow lower on the *pedunculus*, and it blooms fomewhat later.

V. canina, produces a ftem; its flower, which is fometime white, is larger, and does not appear till April.

V. tricolor, is fufficiently diftinguifhed by the colours of the flower, and the oblong fhape of its leaves. Blooms in May.

Nar-

This pale yellow flower, which I ga- *Nar-ciſſus.*
thered at the corner of the wood, you
ſee, has ſix *ſtamina* and one *piſtillum:*
therefore it is of the Claſs *Hexandria*
and of the Order *Monogynia.* The *petela*
are ſix, and the *calyx* is a *ſpatha.* Now
conſult your *Flora Cantabrigienſis,* and
you will find but two *genera* in this
Claſs and Order whoſe *calyx* is a *ſpatha,*
or ſheath, viz. *Allium* and *Narciſſus.* In
the firſt of theſe, the *ſpatha* contains ſeveral flowers: in the plant in your
hand, it includes but one: therefore it
is the latter. And as there is in this
county but one *ſpecies* of this *genus,* you
cannot miſtake in calling it the *Nar-*
ciſſus pſeudo-narciſſus, or Engliſh Daffodil. Mr. Relhan found it at Whitwell,
near Coton, and at Whittlesford.

Linnæus enumerates 14 ſpecies of *Nar-*
ciſſus. In number 61 of the Botanical Ma-
gazine, you will ſee another ſpecies of this
plant, which, the author obſerves, has been
overlooked by Linnæus. He calls it the *in-*
comparabilis, after our ancient botaniſt Par-
kinſon. There is alſo a tolerable wooden
repreſentation of it in Gerarde, who calls

Q   it

it *Narciſſus omnium maximus, ſeu nonpareile.*
It is well known to the London gardeners
by the name of the Egg Narciſſus, or
Orange Phœnix.

Beſides this which I have gathered, there
is a ſpecies, called *poeticus*, found in ſome
parts of this kingdom. It is rather a rare
plant. Its ſpecific appellation you will eaſily
conceive originates in a ſuppoſition that this
is the flower into which the ſelf-enamored
ſon of Cephiſſus was metamorphoſed.

—— crȯceum pro corpore florem
Inveniunt, foliis medium cingentibus albis.

It ſeems, indeed, pretty evident, from the
deſcriptions of Theophraſtus, Dioſcorides
and Pliny, that our Daffodil is a ſpecies of
the Narciſſus of the ancients. There is but
one objection to this ſuppoſition: they do
not, by any means, agree in their time of
flowering. The firſt and laſt of theſe ancient naturaliſts tell us that their Narciſſus
blooms about the Autumnal equinox, and
Virgil's

—————— *nec ſera comantem*
Narciſſus,
I am ſure you remember.

What

What tree, or rather fhrub, is that *Pru-* in the hedge, bearing thofe white blof- *nus.* foms? Let us examine the flower.

The *ftamina*, you perceive, are numerous, 20 or more: therefore it is either of the Clafs *Icofandria* or *Polyandria*. But I have no doubt to which it belongs, when I fee that the *ftamina* are not fixed to the *recep-taculum*, but to the infide of the *calyx*; that circumftance being peculiarly charaƈteriftic of the Clafs *Icofandria*. Befides, the calyx is of one leaf, and the petals are fixed to the fide of it; circumftances which pofi-tively diftinguifh this clafs.

In the centre of thefe *ftamina* you find one *piftillum*: therefore it is of the Order *Mono-gynia*; of which this ifland produces but one genus, viz. *Prunus*. Of this genus I have, in the *Synopfis*, defcribed 5 fpecies, only three of which grow in this part of the kingdom.

In the *infititia* the *pedunculi* grow in pairs, the leaves are oval and a little woolly. In the *ceracius* the flowers grow in a kind of fhort umbell, and the leaves are ovato-lanceolate. But in the *fpinofa* the leaves are lance-fhaped, fmooth, ferrated, the branches fpinous, and the flowers grow from the alæ of the leaves on fingle *pedunculi*; all which

cir-

circumſtances unite in the ſhrub from which you took this bloſſom: therefore it is the *Prunus ſpinola*, Black-thorn, or Sloe.

This claſs *Icoſandria* comprehends many fruit-bearing trees and ſhrubs, none of which are indigenous in this kingdom except the Sloe, the wild Pear, the Crab, the Bramble, the Medlar, the Raſberry, and the *Sorbus*, or Service-tree; that tree of the fruit of which Virgil tells us, the Scythians made a liquor in imitation of wine; that is, a ſort of Cyder. Sitting by a good fire

Hic noctem ludo ducunt, et pocula læti
Fermento atque acidis imitantur vitea ſorbis.

Of theſe trees and ſhrubs, only the firſt four are found wild in Cambridgeſhire.

As this month is not very prolific of flowers in the fields, let us walk down towards yon rivulet. Probably we may find more trees that will bring to your recollection other lines of my favourite Roman poet.

Popu- Thoſe trees growing on the banks
lus. are the *Populus nigra*, Black Poplar: its male and female bloſſoms are on ſeparate trees; conſequently they are of the
Claſs

Clafs *Dioecia*. In the male flower you will find eight *ftamina*; therefore the Order is *Octandria*. The *calyx* of the *amentum* is a lacerated fcale, and the corolla turbinated, oblique and entire. In the female, the *ftigma* is quadrifid; the capfule bilocular, and the feeds numerous and downy: fuch is the generic character. The fpecies is determined by the leaves being of a rhomboidal fhape, dark green and on yellow footftalks.

The Poplar, and probably this fpecies, is among the trees that Virgil fuppofed to grow fpontaneoufly, without feed.

Namque aliæ, nullis hominum cogentibus, ipfæ
Sponte fua veniunt, campofque et flumina late
Curva tenent; ut molle filer, lentæ geniftæ,
Populus, et glauca canentia fronde faliſta.

What this *filer* was, is doubtful. Commentators alfo differ in opinion concerning the *lentæ Geniftæ*. It has generally been tranflated Broom, named *Spartium* by Linnæus, whofe *Genifta* is our Furze or Whin. Virgil in the fame book of his Georgics, mentions the *Genifta* as affording leaves for

the

the cattle, fhade for the fhepherds, hedges for the fields, and food for the bees.

—falices, humilefque geniftæ
Aut illæ pecori frondem, aut paftoribus umbras
Sufficiunt, feptemque fatis, et pabula melli.

Neither of thefe fhrubs feem to anfwer thefe feveral intentions.

Adieu.

L E T.

LETTER XXVII.

APRIL.

PREVIOUS to the confideration of any new plants which we may meet with in this day's ftroll, let us recollect the Claffes and Orders with which you became acquainted in our laft excurfion. Thefe were

Bellis perennis, of the Clafs *Syngenefia* and Order *Polygamia fuperflua*.

Ranunculus ficaria, and *Caltha paluftris* both of the Clafs *Polyandria* and Order *Polygynia*.

Viola odorata, of the Clafs *Syngenefia* and Order *Monogamia*.

Narciffus pfeudo Narciffus, of the Clafs *Hexandria* and Order *Monogynia*.

Prunus fpinofa, of the Clafs *Icofandria* and Order *Monogynia*.

Populus nigra, of the Clafs *Dioecia* and Order *Octandria*.

Thefe feven plants being your firft botanical acquaintance, I hope you will acknowledge them whenever you meet them in future,

Q 4

ture,

ture, and that you will recollect to what Regiment and Company they belong.

Pri-mula.   The pale yellow flowers that so beautifully adorn that bank, are also old acquaintance. You have known them, from a child, to be called Primroses; but their vernacular appellation is all you know of them. Let us first try to discover their Class. Having stripped off the *calyx* and divided the *corolla,* you see, at the bottom of the tube, 5 very short *stamina:* therefore it is of the Class *Pentandria,* and the single *pistillum* in the centre, leaves no doubt as to the order. The *corolla,* you see, is regular, monopetalous, and fixed below the *germen.* The seeds are inclosed in a *capsula.* These circumstances fix it in the second division of this Order. The *genus* is determined by the *involucrum* at the base of the *umbel,* the cylindrical shape of the tube of the *corolla,* and its open mouth; the *species,* by its hairy wrinkled, dentaled leaves, and each stalk bearing but one flower. The down on the calyx and stalk, is longer and thicker than in the Cowslip.

You

You will find a confiderable difference in the opinions of botanical writers concerning this *genus*. In the *Flora Anglica*, and in my *Synopfis*, there are three *Species*, viz. *Primula vulgaris*, Primrofe; *P. veris*, Cowflip; and *P. farinofa*, Bird's-eye. To thefe our friend Relhan adds *P. inodora*, Oxlip, which I have made a variety of *P. veris*. Now Linnæus confiders the Primrofe, the Cowflip and the Oxlip, as varieties of the fame fpecies. Thefe are difagreements that frequently occur among botanical writers, owing to the difficulty of drawing a diftinct line between Species and Variety. Thefe feveral plants, however, whether you call them Species or Varieties, are fo evidently different in appearance, that you can never miftake one for the other.

This Clafs *Pentandria*, the 5th in the Linnæan Syftem, contains the moft plants, except the Clafs *Cryptogamia*. It comprehends 6 Orders, diftinguifhed by the number of the *piftilla*. In the Order in which you found the Primrofe, the plants are arranged according to the number and fituation of the *petala*, and feeds.

That

Alsi-   That trailing plant with small white
ne,   flowers, you tell me, without hesitation,
is common Chickweed. You are pro-
bably right, because there is no other
plant, to which it bears any resem-
blance, yet in bloom; but, next month
you will find other plants, which are
also commonly called Chickweed: they
bear a strong family likeness to this
plant, but are of a different class. The
stamina, you find, are 5, and the *pistilla*
3. The Class and Order therefore are
determined. Turning to your *Synopsis*,
you find in this Order, *Trigynia*, only
four *genera*, three of which are trees,
and the fourth *Alcine media*, the plant
in your hand.

In the Class *Decandria*, there are three genera, viz. *Silene*, *Stellaria* and *Cerastium*, from
several species of which the *Alcine media* is
not easily distinguished. Curtis says, it may
be known from every other plant, by its
petals being shorter than the calyx, and its
stem alternately hairy on one side. Its flowers have been observed to open about 9 in
the morning and to close at noon.

This

This plant, with blue flowers, which *Gle-coma,* I gathered under the hedge, you may possibly know by the smell. However, let us examine it scientifically: the smell may deceive you. If you open the flower, you will discover 4 stamina, two of which are shorter than the other two: therefore the class is *Didynamia,* in which there are but two Orders, viz. *Gymnospermia,* seeds naked, and *Angiospermia,* seeds inclosed in a vessel. Here the seeds are naked, it is therefore of the first of these Orders. If now you observe the *antheræ,* you will see that each pair forms a cross, which is the generic character of the plant *Glecoma;* and as there is but one Species of this *genus,* it can be no other than the *Glecoma hederacea,* or Ground-ivy.

The corolla of the *Glecoma,* you observe, is of a particular and irregular shape: its upper lip stands erect and is divided half-way down; the under, spreads and is cut into three segments, forming a kind of gaping or grinning mouth. Most of the flowers of this Class have the same appearance and are therefore easily known. It comprehends

hends the *Labiati*, lipped; *Verticillati*, whirled; *Perfonatæ*, mafked; and *Ringentes*, grinning flowers of former botanifts. The Balm,
the Mint, the Lavender in our gardens; the
nettles under the hedges, and that *Lamium*,
which you may fafely pull notwithftanding
its refemblance to a nettle, are of this Clafs
and Order.

Lami-   Of thefe *Lamiums* you will find three
um.   Species, viz. *L. album*, *L. purpurium*,
and *L. amplexicaule*. The two firft are
named from the colour of their flowers: confequently, that in your hand is
the white Dead-nettle; which, befides
the colour of its flowers, is diftinguifhed by its leaves being more acute. In
the *amplexicaule*, the upper leaves embrace the ftem, are almoft circular and
deeply notched. You will know thefe
Lamiums from other plants of the fame
Clafs and Order, by the upper lip of
the flower being entire, the lower having two lobes, and a tooth on each fide
the mouth. You will find excellent .
plates of thefe three *Lamiums* in the
Flora Londinenfis,

Now

Now pull me a good specimen of *Chæro-* that umbelliferous plant with white *phyllum.* flowers, that feems to thrive fo well under thefe elms. I have no diffi- culty in telling you its name, without examination, becaufe I know there is no other plant of that kind yet in flower. It is the *Chærophyllum fyl- veftre*, Cow-parfley or wild Cicely, of the Clafs *Pentandria* and Order *Di- gynia*, which Order comprehends, though not exclufively, the *Umbelli- feræ* of Ray and Tournefort. You perceive what is meant by *Umbelli- feræ*. The flowers, you obferve, grow at the end of fpokes, or radii, pro- ceeding from a common centre, each of which centres refts on the extre- mity of another fpoke, alfo proceed- ing from a general centre; fo that it forms a large or general umbel, or umbrella, with a fmall one at the extremity of each radius or rib. The fmall leaves furrounding the root of the umbel, are called the *involucrum:* in the prefent inftance, it belongs to the fmall or partial umbel only, the general umbel having none. The

pre-

prefence or abfence of this *involu-crum*, in plants of this Order, is frequently a very ufeful diftinction; indeed every the moft minute circumftance is neceffary in order to difcriminate thefe umbelliferous plants, which are a numerous tribe and many of them very like each other.

The generic character is: *Involucrum* reflexed, concave; *petala* inflexo-cordate; fruit oblong, fmooth. Specific character: Stem, in the thick part, groved and hairy, a little fwoln and purplifh near the joints; Leaves proceeding from a fhort fheath.

The common height of this plant is about two feet; but there is one now in the walks of Queen's College, that meafures upwards of 4 feet, and is more than half an inch in diameter at the bottom. Three days ago, I met with a fpecimen at the back gate of St. John's, the entire ftem of which was a deep purple. The number of radii are generally 7 or 8: in that which is now growing in Queen's walks, one of the general umbels has eleven. You will find a good engraving of the *Chærophyllum fylveftre* in *Curtis.*

There is another fpecies common in this

king-

kingdom, to which Linnæus has given the fpecific name of *temulum*, for no very obvious reafon. I do not even know the word. Pliny, I remember, ufes *temulentia* for drunkennefs. But we have no bufinefs with this fpecies at prefent, as it will not flower till July.

Look at your watch. Not quite noon. Then we have time fufficient to mount the Hills, where we fhall find an elegant little plant now in bloom, of which my friend Relhan has given an engraving rather too much expanded, but an accurate defcription.

There it is, in great abundance. You have no difficulty in pronouncing it to be of the Clafs *Polyandria* and Order *Polygynia*. You fee it has no calyx, and the petals are 6: therefore it muft be a fpecies of *Anemone*, of which *genus* there are, in this kingdom, but four fpecies, and in Cambridgefhire only two, viz. *A. pulfatilla* and *A. nemorofa*. The firft of thefe is particularly diftinguifhed by its jagged *involucrum*, its ftalk being 8 or 10 inches high, its purple flower, and *foliis bipinnatis*. The flowers in

your

your hand, you see, correfponds exactly with this defcription; you have therefore no doubt that it is the *Anemone pulfatilla*, or Pafque-flower.

Ulmus.   Let us now defcend into the vale.— Thofe trees, in that hedge, which Virgil diftinguifhes for their luxuriant produce of leaves,

——— *fecundæ frondibus Ulmi*,

are now in bloom.   If you examine the flower, you will find 5 *ftamina* and 2 *piftilla*: they are therefore of the Clafs and Order, *Pentandria Digynia*.   You know the *genus* by the *calyx* being fhaped like a top, wrinkled, with 5 fegments and the *ftamina* being double its length.   The fpecies is determined by its leaves being doubly ferrated: befides, it is the only Elm in this country.   Linnæus calls it *Ulmus campeftris*.

Vale.

L E T-

LETTER XXVIII.

MAY.

———— While the rosy-footed May
Steals blushing on, together let us tread
The morning dews, and gather in their prime
Fresh-blooming flowers.

THE first, among the objects of our pursuit, that catches your eye, is that beautifully whitening hedge. *Cratægus.*

The Hawthorn whitens, and the juicy groves
Put forth their buds, unfolding by degrees,
Till the whole leafy forest stands display'd.

The sight of the Hawthorn brought these lines to my memory. I do not repeat them for their beauty: *Juicy* is a vile epithet applied to groves, and the lines are very profaic. Examine one of the flowers, and you will find in it about 20 stamina, which, with the petals, are fixed, not to a *receptaculum*, but to the inside of the calyx: you know it therefore to be of the Class *Icofandria*, and the two styles tell you the Order. But these

R

two

two ftyles, you obferve, are, in fact, the divifions of one *piftillum*. From this circumftance, Dr. Stokes, in Withering's *Botanical
Arrangement,* afferts, that this our common
Hawthorn is the Cratægus *monogyna*, and not
the *oxyacantha* of Linnæus, as Hudfon, Relhan, Lightfoot and I have made it. Dr.
Withering is of Stokes's opinion, and accordingly fubftitutes the *monogyna* for the
oxyacantha. But the fpecific character of the
firft is, *foliis fubtrifidis acutis*; that of the
latter, *foliis obtufis fubtrifidis ferratis:* now the
leaves of our Hawthorn are certainly obtufe
and ferrated. As to the *piftillum*, it is fometimes entire, but more frequently divided
into two ftyles, and fometimes thefe ftyles
are diftinct down to the bottom. Lyons, in
the MS. quoted by Relhan, fays, that the
ftyle is firft fimple and afterwards divided.
I doubt this fact, becaufe I have repeatedly
found the ftyle divided before the expanfion
of the *corolla*.

There are in the laft edition of the *Syftema Vegetabilum,* 15 fpecies of the Cratægus,
only three of which are found in this country, viz. *C. aria,* Whitebeam tree; *C. tormi-
nalis,* Service tree; and *C. oxyacantha,* Hawthorn.

thorn. This is not the firſt ſhrub, or tree (for when it ſtands ſingle it generally de-ſerves the latter appellation) that we have examined belonging to this Claſs *Icoſandria.* In March, you remember, we met with the *Prunus ſpinoſa* in bloſſom; but it is of the Order *Monogynia.*

Let us now examine that yellow *Sina-pis.* flower which grows ſo profuſely among the green corn. The petals of the flower being four, equal, and in the form of a croſs, tell us, at once, that it is of that natural claſs called by Ray, *Siliquoſæ*; by Tournefort, *Cruciformi,* and by Linnæus, *Tetradynamia,* from from Τεσσαρες *quatuor* and Δυναμις *poten-tia.* The *Stamina,* you obſerve, are ſix, four long and two ſhort ones: at the baſe of the latter, there is a nectarife-rous gland, which, that it may not be compreſſed, obliges two of the *ſtamina* to make a curve; this circumſtance ren-ders them ſhorter than the other four. The Orders in this Claſs are *Siliculoſæ,* ſeeds in a broad pod or pouch, and *Siliquoſæ,* ſeeds in a long pod. But theſe diſtinctions are of no uſe in the preſent ſtate of this

 plant.

plant. You will find it however among the *Siliquofæ*, and its expanded calyx, the erect claws of the petals, the gland between the fhort *flamina* and the *piftillum*, and between the longer and the calyx, declare it to be of the genus *Sinapis*.

The *fpecies* are diftinguifhed by the pods; but, as thefe have not yet appeared, we muft find fome other mark. There have been difcovered, in all, 17 different fpecies of *Sinapis*, but three of which grow wild in this kingdom: thefe are *S. nigra*, black Muftard, *S. alba*, white Muftard, and *S. arvenfis*, wild Muftard or Charlock. Now the firft my friend Relhan has thus characterized, *caulis valde remofis, ramis diftantibus expanfis*; which defcription does not apply to the plant in your hand: in the fecond, the leaves are deeply cut and jagged, and the ftem finely groved; befides, neither of thefe bloom in this month; it muft therefore be the *Sinapis arvenfis*. There is another pernicious corn-weed which you will find in flower in July, that much refembles this Charlock: it is the *Raphanus raphaniftrum*; but it is not fo tall a plant, is of a lighter green, the branches are longer in proportion, and the leaves are pinnatifid. The flowers of this *wild Radifh*

are

are fometimes white and fometimes of a pale fleſhcolour, but generally yellow with dark veins.

Here is another weed, with white *Lythof-* flowers, which, on theſe lands, ſeems *permum.* more inimical to the farmer than the Charlock or any other. You will find it of the Claſs *Pentandria* and Order *Monogynia.*

The flower, you obſerve, is monopetalous, regular, and fixed below the germin; the ſeeds are naked, and the leaves are rough: therefore we ſhall find it in the firſt diviſion of the firſt Order of this Claſs. The *corolla,* you ſee, is ſhaped like a funnel, with five ſlight ſegments obtuſe and erect. The tube is cylindrical and open. The *calyx* has 5 diviſions. Now theſe circumſtances unite only in the *genus Lithoſpermum,* of which Linnæus has 8 ſpecies: three of theſe are natives of Britain, but only two have been found in Cambridgeſhire, viz. *L. officinale,* and *L. arvenſe.* The ſtem of the firſt grows to the height of about 2 feet. The plant in your hand is not above half that height. In the firſt the leaves are veined; in this they are not: but the redneſs of the root

R 3   de-

determines your plant to be the *L. arvenfe* or baftard Alkanet. Linnæus fays, the girls in Sweden paint their faces with this root on certain feftivals.

Eryfi-   What is that very upright plant, *mum.* with a fmall white flower, under the hedge? The flower tells you, at once, that it is of the Clafs *Tetradynamia*, and the long pod informs you, that it is alfo of the Order, *Siliquofa*. Now the pods, you obferve, are columnar, and fquare, and the calyx clofed: therefore it is an *Eryfimum*; and, if you rub any part of the plant, the garlic fmell will tell you, that it can be no other than the *E. aliaria*, called *Jack by the hedge* or *Sauce alone*. It is diftinguifhed from other fpecies of *Eryfimum*, by its heart-fhaped leaves. It grows to the height of 2 or 3 feet. The ftem is round, fmooth, branched towards the top; branches alternate, erect, and the flow-ers fmall and terminal, as you fee.

Carda-   Thofe purple-white flowers that *mine.* are fprinkled on that meadow, are of the fame Clafs and Order as the laft, laſt. The Latin name is *Cardamine pratenſis*, and the Engliſh, *Ladies-ſmock*. This reminds you of Shake-ſpear's ſong in *Love's Labour loſt*,

When daizies pied and violets blue,
And Lady-ſmocks all ſilver white,
And Cuckow buds of yellow hue
Do paint the meadows with delight.

You will find theſe lines quoted by *Curtis* in the *Flora Londinenſis*, and a very neat plate of the flower; but he makes no comment on the lines, which ſeem to want ſome explanation. I have never yet met with any *ſilver-white* Lady-ſmocks: they have always a conſiderable tinge of red or purple. As to the *Cuckow-buds of yellow hue*, it is difficult to aſcertain the flower meant by the poet. It evidently was not the *Lych-nis-floſcuculi*, which we call Cuckow-flower; for that is red, as you will ſee: we ſhall pro-bably meet with it in the next meadow.

I fancy theſe *Cuckow-buds of yellow hue*, were the common Butter-cups that ſo de-lightfully paint this luxuriant meadow. There is indeed no other flower that may with eqaul propriety be ſaid to paint the meadows yellow: beſides, the flower of this

Ra-

Ranunculus, before it expands, has the appearance of 'a bud. Are they not called Cuckow-buds in Staffordshire?

But to return to our *Cardamine pratensis.* It is the only species of this *genus* found near Cambridge. It is distinguished by its leaves being pinnated, and the *folioli* of the radical leaves being roundish, whilst those on the stem are lance-shaped. The generic character is—Pod bursting, the valves then rolling back: *Stigma* entire; *calyx* a little open.

There are in all 15 species of *Cardamine,* six of which are indigenous in Britain.

Vicia. That plant with papilionaceous purple flowers, climbing up the hedge, is obviously of the Class *Diadelphia,* and the number of its *stamina* will tell you, that it is of the Order *Decandria.* Now take off the *corolla,* and you will discover that the summit of the *pistillum,* called the *stigma,* is transversely bearded. This minute peculiarity determines its generic name to be *Vicia;* and, that it is the species *sativa,* I conclude from its flowers growing in pairs, its leaves consisting of about six pair of wings and

and terminating in a divided tendril; but the burnt spot under the *stipulæ* leaves no doubt that it is the common Vetch or Tare, which, you remember, Virgil mentions among the pulse which are supposed so to fertilize the ground as to render fallowing unnecessary.

Aut ubi flava seres, mutato sidere, farra,
Unde prius lætum siliqua quaßente legumen,
Aut tenues fætus Viciæ, tristisque lupini
Sustuleris fragiles calamos, sylvamque sonantem.

Do not you think that *sidere*, in the first line, should be *semine?*

Suppose we now examine one of these *Ranunculi*, commonly called Crowfeet or Butter-cups. You perceive immediately that it is of the Class *Polyandria* and Order *Polygynia*. Its *calyx* consists of 5 leaves, and its *corolla* of 5 petals, with a melliferous pore at the base of each; the seeds are naked. These particulars form the essential generic character of *Ranunculi*. As to its species, the retroflected *calyx*, the sulcated *pedunculus*, the stalk erect, bearing many flowers,

*Ranun-
culus.*

flowers,

flowers, the bulbous root, and particularly its being now in bloom in
this dry meadow, leave no doubt
that it is the *Ranunculus bulbosus*, or
bulbous Crowfoot.

Of this *genus* there are no lefs than 44
different fpecies, 14 of which are natives of
this ifland. That yellow flower, which you
fee on the fwamp, is one of them: its trivial
name is *feleratus*, from the refemblance of
its lower leaves to thofe of Celery. It is
very eafily diftinguifhed by the remarkable
thicknefs of its ftem, which is hollow like
a reed; by its minute flowers, and the
conical fhape of the *receptaculum*. This
fpecimen, you fee, is full two feet high. It
feldom grows fo tall.

Look this way and you will fee among
that corn, a moft plentiful crop of other
Ranunculi. Thefe, you obferve, have alfo a
fmall flower, but of a paler yellow and numerous. The leaves are deeply divided and
fubdivided, fo as to form a number of narrow ftraps. This circumftance, and its
prickly feeds conftitute its fpecific character.
Its common height is about a foot, though
that you have gathered meafures 17 or 18
inches. It is the *Ranunculus arvenfis*.

On

On this turf, between the corn- *Orchis.*
lands, you fee fcattered a few beautiful purple flowers, which, at a
diftance, look fomewhat like garden
hyacinths. But, you now perceive,
that the *corolla* is of a very different
fhape. It refembles no flower that
we have hitherto examined.

As it is neceffary to begin your inveftigation by afcertaining the Clafs, you muft diveft the plant of its petals. You now difcover that the *ftamina* are fixed to the *ftylus*,
or rather to a *nectarium* which fupplies the
place of a *piftillum*. Your plant therefore
is of the 20th Clafs, *Gynandria*, for a particular defcription of which I refer you to
your *Clavis*. The *ftamina* are two, therefore
it is the firft Order, *Diandria*; for in this
Clafs, the Orders depend on the number of
Stamina, and not on the *Piftilla*, as in many
of the preceding Claffes.

Now as to the *genus*, you fee there is a
nectarium, in the fhape of a horn, behind
the flower. This circumftance tells you
that it muft be an *Orchis*, and the undivided
bulbs of its root; quadrifid, fcallopped lip
of the *nectarium*; the obtufe afcending horn,
and the obtufe conniving petals, convince
you,

you, that it is the *Orchis morio*, or Meadow Orchis. The *genera* in this Order are dif-tinguiſhed by the ſhape of the *nectarium*.

Of this *genus* there are in all 50 ſpecies, ten of which have been found in Britain. You will find a good engraving of this plant in the *Flora Londinenſis*.

Vale.

LETTER XXIX.

JUNE.

Nunc frondent sylvæ, nunc formosissimus annus.

TO speak in the language of a sportf-
man, this month will afford us ample diverfion. We fhall find no lack of
Game. Herbarizing may indeed, with fome
propriety, be compared with the amufements
of the chafe. A botanift is continually hunting; but with this very great advantage,
that his fport is unmixed with cruelty. Happily the objects of his purfuit have no feel-
ing: they are unconfcious of their exiftence,
to deprive them of it, therefore, cannot be
attended with remorfe.

Pull that yellow flower with two heads.
Each head, you perceive, is a clufter of diftinct florets of what is called a papilonace-
ous fhape. You conclude, therefore, that
we muft look for it in the Clafs *Diadelphia*.
Indeed this butterfly-appearance of the
flower is a much more obvious and invariable criterion of the Clafs, than the *ftamina*
being united in two fets, or brotherhoods
as the title implies; but Linnæus's fyftem
would

would not suffer him to make the *corolla* characteristic of a Class. It is however a perfectly natural Class, comprehending the *Papilionacei* of Tournefort, the *Irregulares tetrapetali* of Rivinus, and the *Ligumenofæ* of Ray.

An-thyllis. Almost all the plants of this Class are of the Order *Decandria*; you will accordingly, on a minute inspection, find ten *stamina* in each of those small flowers. In running over the generic characters, there is nothing to cause any hesitation till you come to *Anthyllis: calyx ventricosus*; but the *calyx* in this genus is not only ventricose, but woolly. This agrees well with the plant you have gathered; and, in the specific character of the only species in this kingdom, Linnæus says, *foliis pinnatis inæqualibus, capitulo duplicato.* These circumstances may convince you, that you hold in your hand the *Anthyllis vulneraria,* or Ladies-finger. If you have any doubt, I must refer you to Relhan's very accurate description of this species; where among other marks of distinction, you will find —

Caules

Caules teretes, pubescentes. Flores sessiles in majori capitulo 20. *Corolla flava.* Now I hope you are satisfied.

There is a shrub in that hedge that will remind you of a line in the second Georgic. *Cor-nus.*

At myrtus validis hastibus, et bona bello Cornus.

Examine the flower. *Tetrandria Monogynia.* The coralla, you observe, stands above the germen, and consists of four regular petals. Now turn over your *Synopsis.* You find it must be in the fourth division. The first plant is the *Cornus,* with an *involucrum* of 4 leaves, and a *perianthium* of one, with 4 teeth. The *corolla* is less than the *involucrum,* and shorter than the *stamina.* These essentials quadrate with that flower: therefore you can have no doubt as to the *genus;* and as you learn, from your *Flora Cantabrigiensis,* that there is but one Species in this county, your shrub must necessarily be the *Cornus sanguinea,* or Dogberry; a shrub which merits some veneration, were it only for being Godfather to an admirable character in *Much-ado about nothing.* Honest Taswell! *I ne'er shall look upon thy like again!*

Gar-

Garrick in Benedick was not a jot fuperior to Tafwell in Dogberry. With what genuine appearance of ftupid fimplicity he exclaimed —*O that he were here to write me down an afs!*

But to return to our *Cornus.* It is certain, that the Romans made their fpears of Myrtle and Cornel, though, from a paffage quoted by Martyn in his Commentary on the Georgics, it appears that Pliny preferred the Afh.

Coni-um. That tall umbelliferous plant, with dark-green gloffy fubdivided leaves, and white flowers, claims your particular attention. It is the famous Hemlock, which on the credit of Profeffor Storck of Vienna, was fuppofed an infallible cure for cancers. The number of *ftamina* and *piftilla* declare it to be of the Clafs and Order *Pentandria, Digynia.* Its former generic name was *Cicuta,* but Linnæus chufes to call it *Conium,* and *maculatum,* from the fpots on the ftem. Why this *Cicuta* of all other botanifts, muft have its ancient name taken from it and transferred to a different plant, I do not comprehend:

nor

nor do I know where he got the word *Conium*; unlefs from Pliny, who, I think, mentions it as the name of a town in Phrygia. This our Hemlock was certainly the *Cicuta* of which the pipe prefented by Menalcas to the fhepherd Mopfis, was made.

Hæc te nos fragili donabimus ante cicuta.

I myfelf, when a boy, have often made pipes of it: they had but few notes indeed, but the tone was not unlike that of the Clarionet.

This *Conium macalatum* is diftinguifhed from other plants of the fame Clafs and Order, by the *involucella* extending only half round the fpoke on which it ftands, and confifting generally of three leaves, or rather of 3 divifions of one leaf; and by the fhape of the feed, which is nearly fpherical, with 5 ftriæ, and notched at each end. There are four *fpecies* of this *genus*, but the *maculatum* only is indigenous in Britain. You may eafily know it by the brown fpots on the ftem, and the gloffy dark-green leaves. You fee it is a tall plant: this fpecimen meafures, at leaft, 5 feet.

S

There

Sambucus. There is a large plant with a bufhy purplifh flower, under that hedge. It bears fome refemblance, both in leaf and bloffom, to the common Elder-tree. It is indeed very nearly allied to it. We call it in Englifh, Dwarf Elder, or Danewort, becaufe, we are told, that it firft fprang up in this kingdom from the blood of the Danes that were maffacred here. It is the *Sambucus ebulus*, with the purple juice of whofe berries, Pan, in Virgil's tenth Eclogue, is fuppofed to have fmeared his face.

Pan deus Aracadiæ venit, quem vidimus ipfi,
Sanguineis Ebuli baccis minioque rebentem.

If you examine the flowers, you will find it to be of the Clafs and Order *Pentandria Trigynia*, and of that divifion in which the *corolla* ftands above the germen. Its generic character is — *Calyx* and *Corolla* of 5 fegments; berry containing three feeds. As to the fpecies, there can be no difficulty, becaufe there are but two, and one of thefe is a tree. You will find a good engraving of this plant in the *Flora Londinenfis.*

Now

Now turn your attention to thofe *Medica-* yellow flowers, like fmall buttons, *go.* that grow fo plentifully among the grafs. It fomewhat refembles the flower of the Hop, but is much lefs. You would fuppofe it a Trefoil: it is indeed naturally of that family: it is a *Medicago,* which differs from the *genus* Trifolium in the *carina* of the *corolla* being preffed down from the *vexillum,* and particularly in its pod being compreffed and fpiral. The fhape of the florets that compofe thefe yellow heads, and the number of very minute *ftamina* will inform you that it is of the Clafs and Order *Diadelphia Decandria,* and the fpecies, *lupulina,* is determined by the fpikes being oval, the pods reniform, containing a fingle feed, and the ftems trailing. Former botanifts called this plant *Medica:* Linnæus chofe to call it *Medicago.*

Whether Virgil meant this fpecies may be doubtful: however the *Medica* is among the plants which he advifes to be fown in the Spring.

Vere

Vere favis satio; tum te quoque Medica putres
Accipiunt sulci.

Pliny says it was called *Medica*, from Media the country whence it was brought into
Greece:—*Medica externa, etiam Græciæ, ut
a Medis advecta per bella Persarum, quæ Da-
rius intulit*—If you be curious to know
more of this plant, I refer you to Martyn's
Georgics. He thinks Virgil meant our
Lucern.

Hyoscya-
mus.

You observe, among that rubbish,
a large plant, with dark buff-co-
loured flowers of a singular appearance. You find it has five *stamina*
and one *pistillum:* you have therefore no doubt as to the Class and
Order. The *corolla* is funnel-shaped
and obtuse; the *stamina* are inclined,
and the *capsula* is bilocular and covered. It is therefore an *Hyoscyamus;*
and though there be seven *species* of
this *genus,* yet as the *niger* is the
only species in this kingdom, it can
be no other than our common Henbane. It is very easily known by the
mixture of deep purple and buff in
the

the flower. The Henbane is generally confidered as a poifonous plant. It was fome time ago recommended as a fubftitute for *opium*.

That humble yellow flower, which *Potentilla.* adorns the fides of this path, I fuppofe, you confider, as a common *butter-cup*, beneath your notice. But you will find, on examination, that it belongs to a very different Clafs: and furely its beautiful filver-feathered leaves merit fome attention. The *ftamina* you find are about twenty. Hence you might doubt whether it does not belong to the Clafs *Polyandria*; but if you examine the five petals, you will find that they are fixed, not to a *receptaculum*, but to the *calyx*, which is monopetalous; fo that it is of the Clafs *Icofandria*. Now you obferve in the centre of the flower, a numerous collection of fmall buds, forming a knob, with ftyles: therefore it is of the Order *Polygynia*. The leaves, you fee, are pinnated, and ferrated; the ftem creeps, and the ftalk bears a fingle

flower.

flower, To this we may add, from Relhan, that there are from ten to twelve pair of wings in each leaf, decreafing in fize towards each extremity. Thefe circumftances, with the filver whitenefs of the under fide of the leaves, leave no doubt that it is the *Potentilla anferina*, or Silver Weed, called alfo wild Tanfey.

Scandix. You obferve, among the corn, a weed with a fmall white flower, and feveral long beaks, which you muft fuppofe contain the feeds of the plant. By thefe long beaks you will eafily diftinguifh it in future, Its generic name is *Scandix*, and from the fuppofed fimilitude to the teeth of a comb, the fpecific appellation is *pecten*. Our botanical predeceffors have called it Shepherd's-needle, or Venus-comb. If you examine the flower, you will find it of the Clafs *Pentandria* and Order Dygynia. Thefe teeth of the comb are generally about an inch in length. Probably the combs of the ancients were of a rude conftruction.

Vale,

L E T-

LETTER XXX.

JUNE.

LET us take this left hand road to *Li-num.* the Hills: we shall probably meet with some new objects.—That upright slender plant, with a single simple stem, thick set with very small pointed leaves, and terminated by a tuft of beautiful blue flowers, is the *Linum perenne*, or perenniel blue Flax. The five petals will fall off almost as soon as you touch them. You will then discover five *stamina* and the same number of *pistilla*. *Pentandria Pentagynia*, therefore, is the Class and Order. That it is a *Linum*, I know, from its pentaphyllous *calyx*, its pentapetalous *corolla*, its quinquevalve capsule, and its solitary seeds; and, that it is the *perenne*, I learn, from the segments of the calyx being obtuse, the leaves on the stem numerous, small, alternate, and by the flowers growing in a tuft.

We have, in Britain, five species of *Linums*, as you will find in your *Synopsis*. No. 1.

usi-

ufitatiffimum, grows to the heighth of three feet, its ftem is branched, and each branch terminated by a blue flower. No. 2. is the plant in your hand. No. 3. *tenuefolium*, is diftinguifhed by its ligneous, numerous ftems, and a fmaller flower. No. 4. *cathar-ticum*, is a fmaller plant, with four or five bent ftems, with leaves diftant and oppofite. Its flowers are white and minute. No. 5. *radiola* has four *ftamina* and the fame num-ber of *piftilla*, and therefore belongs to an-other Clafs.

The ancients were univerfally of opinion that a crop of Flax impoverifhes the ground. I am fure you recollect this line in the firft book of the Georgics.

Urit enim Lini campum feges, urit avenæ.

Hedy-farum.   You obferve there a flower of a full flefh-colour, growing on a long ftalk. You perceive it is formed by a number of florets imbricated fo as, in fome degree, to refemble the head of a cock. Our botanical predecef-fors have therefore called it Cock's-head. It is the *Hedyfarum onobrychis.* From the external appearance of the
blossom,

blossom, you pronounce it to be of the Class *Diadelphia*; and, if you examine the stamina, you will place it in the Order *Decandria*. But, on a more minute investigation, you will be surprised to find only two petals in the flower, viz. the *vixillum* and the *carina*, and that there is no appearance of wings. Neverthelefs, if you apply your glafs, you will difcover two minute, pale flesh-coloured *alæ*, which, in compliance with this artificial fyftem, may be tranflated *wings*.

This *genus* of *Hedyfarum* depends on the *carina* being tranfverfe and obtufe, and on there being a fingle feed in each joint of the pod. There are in all no lefs than *67 fpecies* of this *genus*, only one of which is found on this ifland. It is particularly diftinguifhed from the reft, among thofe with pinnated leaves, by its elongated ftem; but this ftem is rather a long *fcapus* or ftalk, proceeding from a fhort *caulis*, or ftem. For a definition of thefe terms I refer you to your *Clavis*.

There

Poly-gala.   There is a humble plant, growing in patches, with a blue flower, that merits your attention; becaufe it is the only *genus* indigenous in this kingdom, of the Order *Octandria* in the Clafs *Diadelphia.* It is the *Polygala vulgaris,* or Milkwort. It grows, you fee, fomewhat in the manner of that Thyme, its frequent companion on thefe hills; from which however it differs effentially, as you will find when we have examined them both.

Having now, by infpecting the ftamina, determined the Clafs and Order, and knowing that in thefe there is but one fpecies of one genus, difcovered in this kingdom, you know the plant without either generic or fpecific defcription. For greater certainty, however, you may obferve, that the *calyx* is pentaphyllous, and that two of its leaves look like coloured wings. The ftem, you fee, is proftrate, branched, curved and from 4 to 6 inches in length.

Thy-mus.   It is now *time* (without a pun) to take notice of its neighbour, the *Serpyllum* of all the Botanifts before Haller,

who,

who, I believe, firft called it *Thymus*. The *ftamina*, you obferve, are four, two long and two fhort; therefore it is of the Clafs *Didynamia*, and the feeds being naked tells the Order to be *Gymnofpermia*. The generic character is a very fhort one—*Calycis bilabiati faux villis claufa*, and it is fufficiently diftinguifhed from the only other *fpecies*, in this kingdom, by its flowers being collected in a head; thofe of the *acinos*, or Bafil Thyme, are verticillate.

This Thyme, you know, both Greek and Latin poets fuppofed the favorite food of bees. Virgil therefore mentions it as a proper herb to be planted near the hives.

Hæc circum Cafiæ verides, et olentia late Syrpylla.

This *Syrpyllum* of the Romans was the ἕρπυλλον of the Greeks, derived from ἕρπω, to creep. Thefe Romans, as Martyn obferves, frequently changed the Greek afpiration into S, from ἕρπω forming *ferpo*, from ἓξ fex, &c. But Virgil, both in his Eclogues and Georgics, mentions alfo *Thymus*, which Linnæus adopts as the name of the genus.

Dum

Dum juga montis aper, fluvios duin pifcis amabit,
Dumque Thymo pafcentur apes, dum rore cicadæ,
Semper honos, nomenque tuum, laudefque manebunt.

Thefe beautiful lines, you remember, are at the conclufion of the very fublime *apo-theofis* of Daphnis, fuppofed to be Julius Cæfar, fung by Menalcas in the fifth Eclogue: and, in the fourth Georgic,

Ipfe Thymum pinofque ferens de montibus altis
Tecta ferat late circum, cui talia curæ.

This *Thymum* of Virgil is fuppofed to be, not our common Thyme, cultivated in our gardens as a pot-herb, but that fpecies which Ray calls *Thymum legitimum*; that fpecies to the abundance of which Sicily owed its celebrity for its honey, and which is found by travellers in every part of Greece —*Bollonia auctore,* fays Ray, *ita frequens in tota Grecia reperitur, ut nulla herba in montibus facilius proveniat.*

The-fium.   That diffufe plant with fmall whitifh flowers on loofe leafy panicles, is the *Thefium linophyllum,* of which, as a rare plant, Relhan has given a plate. Its Englifh name is baftard Toadflax. You
will

will find, it has no *corolla*; the flower consisting of a *calyx* only, into which the five *stamina* are inserted.

Not far from us, I perceive another scarce plant, of which my friend Relhan has given a plate and an accurate description, in his excellent *Flora Cantabrigiensis*. I mean that diminutive chap, about five inches high, with a yellow star-flower. It is the *Cineraria alpina*, or Mountain Ragwort. There are some doubts about the proper *genus* of this herb; but Linnæus has declared that it is a Proteus of a plant. It is of the Class and Order, *Syngenesia Polygamia superflua*. The flowers, you observe, grow in a loose irregular kind of umbel, and the leaves on the stem are lance-shaped, woolly, and very erect.

It is now time to descend the Hills,

—jam summa procul villarum culmina fumant,
Majoresque cadunt altis de montibus umbræ.

Our rout lies through Cherry Hinton, a village celebrated in the annals of Botany, by having been the scene of our indefatigable Ray's frequent herbarizations; particularly in a field called the *Chalk-pit close*, where
Rel-

Relhan firſt ſhewed me the *Athamanta libanotis*; a ſcarce plant, which, ſince the time
of Ray, had been entirely loſt. We ſhall
viſit this field another time.

You are delighted with the fragrant efflu-
via of this narrow lane. It is the fragrance
of roſes. That ſhrub, with white flowers,
is the *Viburnum opulus*, or Guelder Roſe; and
the other is the *Roſa canina*, or Dog Roſe.
If you examine the *cymæ* of the firſt, you
will find that the ſmall flowers in the centre
have five *ſtamina* and three minute ſtigmata,
and that the large flowers in the *radius* have
neither.

The *Roſa canina* is of the Claſs *Icoſandria
Polygynia*. You will find, in your *Synopſis*,
that it is of the firſt *genus* in that Order, and
that there are five ſpecies in this iſland.

Lotus. There is a yellow flower that we
have frequently ſeen in our walks, but
of which we have hitherto taken no
notice. By the leaves you would ſuppoſe it a Trefoil. Indeed its Engliſh
name is Birdsfoot Trefoil. Linnæus
calls it *Lotus corniculatus*. You will determine the genus by its turbular *calyx*,
the wings of the *corolla* conniving longitudinally

gitudinally upwards, and, hereafter, by
the pod being cylindrical, ftiff, and
longer than the *calyx*. We have but
one fpecies of this genus, which is
characterized by the flatnefs of the
heads, and the ftem being decumbent.
You will find a good plate of this plant
in *Curtis*.

Thofe fine fcarlet, and thofe tall *Papaver.*
blue flowers, equal in colour to the
beft *ultramarine*, and which add fo
much to the beauty of this field of
green corn, are too confpicuous to
pafs unnoticed. The fcarlet flower,
you tell me, is a Poppy.—It is fo;
but I wifh to know fomething more
about it. The *ftamina*, you perceive,
are numerous, and there is, in the
centre, a *germen* covered by a *ftigma*,
but no *ftylus*. Hence I know the
Clafs and Order to be *Polyandria
Monogynia*. The generic character
is—*calyx* diphyllus; *corolla* tetrape-
tala; *capfula* unilocularis, fub ftig-
mate perfiftente poris dehifcens. The
plant you have gathered is the *Papaver rhæas*; it is particularly diftinguifhed

guiſhed from the other three red
Poppies, which alſo grow in corn-
fields and bloom at the ſame time,
by its round ſmooth head, hairy ſtem
and pinnatifid leaves.

We have in this kingdom ſix ſpecies of
Papaver, one of which has white and another yellow flowers. I doubt whether any
of thoſe be the ſort that was ſown for ſome
purpoſe or other, by the ancients, and which,
Virgil ſays, burns the land,

Urunt lethæo perfuſa papavera ſomnö.

Centau-
rea.   That tall plant with the beautiful
blue flower, you will find, is of the
Claſs and Order *Polygamia Fruſtrania.*
The *floſculi* that form the *radius*, you
perceive, have no *ſtigma*, and for
that reaſon can produce no ſeed; they
are therefore of no uſe in the propagation of the plant: that operation is performed by the florets of
the diſk, which are hermaphrodite.
—Having thus aſcertained the Claſs
and Order, conſult your *Synopſis*, and
you will have no doubt of the *genus*,
Centaurea being the only genus indigenous

genous in Britain. As to the *species*, it is evidently the *cyanus*, or blue-bottle, becaufe there is no other with a blue flower.

There is, on the verge of thofe lands, another ftately plant with blue flow-ers, of which probably you have never heard the name. It is a handfome flower to look at, but not very pleafant to touch; its ftem being thick fet with white briftles, each of which, you will perceive, grows on the centre of a brown tubercle. Its five red *ftamina* and forked *piftillum*, are eafily feen, as they project much beyond the rim of the *corolla*. Its common height is about two feet. The flowers, you fee, crowd all to one fide of the fpike, which is generally from fix to nine inches in length. The leaves on the ftem are feffile, hairy and fpear-fhaped. Thefe together are fufficient marks of diftinc-tion. It is the *Echium vulgare*, or Vi-per's Buglos. But I muft apprife you that the flowers on the fpike being la-teral, that is, growing all on one fide, *Echi-um.*

T

is

is fo far from being general, that they more commonly form a regular pyramid.

Liguf-trum.   In that hedge you obferve a fhrub with a white flower, which I dare fay you know to be the Privet, having often feen it form a regular hedge in gardens; to which purpofe it is indeed well adapted. You will find it in the *Synopfis*, the firft *genus* in the Clafs and Order, *Diandria*, Monogynia: accordingly, you fee, in the flower two *ftamina* and one *piftillum.* The generic name is *Liguftrum* and the fpecific *vulgare.* The word *Liguftrum* reminds you of thefe lines in Virgil,

O formofe puer, nimium ne crede colori :
Alba Liguftra cadunt, vaccinia nigra leguntur.

It is however by no means certain, that thefe *alba liguftra* of Virgil were what we call Privet: on the contrary, many commentators are of opinion, that our *Convolvulus fepium*, Great Bindweed, is the plant; and they incline to this opinion from the extreme

extreme whitenefs of the flower and the fuppofed derivation of *Liguftrum* from *li-gando*. Pliny pofitively fays it is a tree: but Pliny was a mere tranfcriber, and, I am,

dear Charles,

Your, &c.

LET-

LETTER XXXI.

JULY.

" What calm joy can this exceed,
This of roving o'er the mead?
Where the hand of Flora pours
Sweeteft voluntary flow'rs:
Where the Zephyr's balmy gale
Wantons in the charming vale."

Vero-
nica. THAT plant, with thefe beautiful china-blue flowers, which grows fo luxuriantly in the brook, is the *Veronica beccabunga*, commonly called Brooklime. It is of the Clafs *Diandria* and Order *Monogynia*. The flowers, you fee, are *inferi, monopetali, et irregulares*. Both *calyx* and *corolla* are quadripartite, and, of the latter, the loweft fegment is the narroweft: thefe particulars determine the *genus*. The *fpecies* is known by its loofe lateral fpikes of blue flowers, its creeping ftem, and by its leaves being thick, feffile, oval, oppofite and notched.

That

That very common plant with large *Mal-* flowers, that grows so plentifully on *va.* each side of this road, you know, I make no doubt, is a species of Mallow. It merits your attention as an example of the Class and Order *Monadelphia Poly-andria*, in which the classical character may be distinctly observed without the help of your glass. You see there are many *stamina* united below in one body or brotherhood. The *corolla* consists of five petals. The calyx is double, with but three leaves in the exterior range, by which last circumstance it is distinguished from the *genus* Althea. We have in this kingdom four species of Malva, viz. *rotundifolia, parviflora, moschata* and *sylvestris*, which last is the plant you have pulled, and which is distinguished from the other three, by its leaves being waved, in 5 or 7 lobes, obtuse, serrated and their foot-stalks hairy.

Here is a plant about two feet in *Sal-* height, with a small blue flower, from *via.* the gaping appearance of which, you suppose it to be of the Class *Didynamia;*

T 3

but

but its unfortunate want of two more ſtamina, ſeparates it from its family. If you examine the flower, you will find it contains one piſtillum and two very diſtinct *ſtamina* with large *antheræ*, which you perceive have burſt longitudinally on the under ſide, and are now in the act of diſcharging, in great profuſion, a fine yellow *pollen*, on the ſummit of the *piſtillum*; but, being naturally taller than the *ſtamina*, it bends its neck down between the ſtamina, for the purpoſe of receiving this yellow duſt. Yet Linnæus, as a generic character ſays—*Filamenta tranſverſe pedicello affixa*; and Dr. Withering tells us, that the rudiments of two chives appear in the mouth of the bloſſom, but they have no tips. In this ſpecies, however, nothing can be more conſpicuous than the ſtamina and *tips*, as he chuſes to call them; and, as to the filaments fixed tranſverſely to a pedicle, there is not the leaſt appearance of it. In this *ſpecies*, you obſerve, the flowers grow in whirls, ſix in each; the leaves are wrinkled, ſcallopped and ſerrated, on the upper part of the ſtem ſeſſile, on

the

the lower on pedicles. The ſtem is quadrangular and *brachiatus*. Relhan ſays it ſmells like black currants: to me, it has rather a mixt pot-herb ſmell. It is the *Salvia verbenaca*, Wild Sage, or Clary. There is another ſpecies, viz. *S. pratenſis*, found in other counties, which is rather a ſcarce plant. This *Salvia verbenaca* you will find, in great plenty, in the field path oppoſite the horſe-bridge of Trinity College.

In that ditch I ſee an umbelliferous *Apium.* plant, which, if you can get at it without a plunge, you will find to be of the Claſs and Order *Pentandria Digynia.*—It is the *Apium graveolens*, the eſſential character of which *genus* is, Seeds oval and ſtriated; *involucrum* of one leaf: petals equal. But ſeeds yet there are none, and as to the *involucrum* according to its arrangement in the *Syſtema Vegetabilium*, it ought to have none. You may, however, diſtinguiſh it by the general umbel conſiſting of few *radii* and the partial of many. Linnæus dertermines the *ſpecies* by the leaves on them being wedge-ſhaped.

T 4

We

We call it, in its wild ſtate, Smallage;
in our gardens Cellery. It is probably
the ελειοσελινον of the Greeks; for their
σελινον the Latin writers always tranſlate *apium.* From the ſituation in
which you have found it, we may, I
think, rationally ſuppoſe it to be Virgil's *Apium.*

Quoque modo potis gauderent intuba rivis,
Et virides apio ripæ ——

Cichori-
um. There grows the very *Intubum* juſt
mentioned. I mean that plant with
large blue flowers, like wheels, growing, without foot-ſtalks, on the ſide
of a zig-zag ſtem, which is firm and
about two feet high. If you examine the calyx you will find it double; the interior formed of 8 ſcales,
the exterior of 5, which are fringed.
The petals are in number from 16
to 20, with 5 notches at the extremity of each. *Linnæus* calls it *Ci-*
chorium intybus. It is of the Claſs
and Order *Syngeneſia Polygamia æqua-*
lis: in Engliſh, Succory. I take it
to be the ſpecies of σερις, which Dioſcorides

corides calls πικρίς. It is certainly the weed, injurious to the farmer, which Virgil fo drolly links with the geefe and cranes.

—— *nihil improbus anfer*
Stramoniæque grues, et amaris Intuba fibris
Officiunt.——

Poffibly it was this fpecies of *cichorium* that made a part of Horace's fallad,

—— *Me pafcunt olivæ,*
Me cichorea, levefque malvæ.

And that, by *olivæ*, he meant the oil which he eat with it. But it is more probable, I think, that he fpeaks of the *Cichorium endivia*, the plant which we call Endive: and yet, if he could eat mallows, he might alfo eat Succory.

Near the plant you have juft ex-amined, there is another more univer-fally common, and which, as you will find in your *Synopfis*, immediately follows the *Cichorium*. It is the *Arctium lappa* of Linnæus, our Burdock, or Clotbur; the famous *Bardana* of the famous Dr. Hill. *Arctium* is the ancient

cient name by which it was called by
Dioscorides. Later botanists have given
it the name of *Lappa*, probably from
λαμβανω, *capio*, from its catching hold
of people's garments as they pass. Linnæus took the Dioscordian name for
the *genus*, and *Lappa* for the *species*. It
is of the Class and Order *Syngenesia*,
Polygamia æqualis. Its *medium* height
is between two and three feet. The
flowers are purple, on the top of a
large, globular imbricated common
calyx, the exterior scales of which are
sharp and hooked, so as to catch fast
hold of every thing they touch. Whether Virgil, enumerating the weeds
that infest the corn-fields, meant this
Burdock, or the *Galium aparine*, is matter of contention among his commentators,

—— *subit aspera sylva,*
Lappæque, Tribulique —— Geor. I. 52.

Be this as it may, the *Lappa* of Pliny is
certainly the *Aparine* of Theophrastus and
Dioscorides. You will find this subject
learnedly discussed in Martyn's Virgil.

You

You look inquifitively for the caufe *Gali-*
of the fweet honey-like fmell you per- *um.*
ceive. It proceeds from thofe fpikes of
fmall yellow flowers that border this
field. If you apply your glafs to any
one of them, you will find it is of the
Clafs and Order *Tetrandria Monogynia.*
The *calyx*, you obferve, is fmall, of one
leaf, with four teeth; the *corolla* monopetalous, plane, without tube, divided
into four fharp fegments. The fruit
confifts of two dry berries, containing
each a fingle feed: therefore it is a *Ga-*
lium. The branches which fupport the
fmall fpikes are very fhort. The leaves
on the ftem grow in whirls, are fhort,
linear, fharp, brittle, fulcated, and eight
or nine in number. The ftem is brown
and fquare: therefore it is the *Galium*
verum, Ladies Bedftraw, or Cheefe-ren-
ning.

We are told by Mr. Pennant and by Mr.
Lightfoot, that in the ifles of Jura, Uift,
Lewis, &c. they ufe the root of this plant
for dying red, and that a decoction of the
flowers is ufed in the ifle of Aran, and in
Chefhire, to curdle milk for cheefe. You
will

will find an excellent engraving of this plant in the *Flora Londinensis*.

We have hitherto taken no notice of that prolific tribe of plants to which, we of the temperate zone, are principally obliged for a confiderable part of our food, our raiment, and for this perpetual verdure, fo grateful to the eye. I need not tell you, that I mean the Graffes. You will probably afcribe our neglect of them to their not bearing flowers, which have always been the objects of our enquiry. But this is not true. Their flowers indeed are neither large not gaudy; neverthelefs it is from their parts of fructification, as in other plants, that they are claffed in the Linnæan fyftem. They are difficult of inveftigation, becaufe the effential parts are fo minute as to require good glaffes, and more time than you can now fpare: for this reafon, we have fuffered the Graffes to pafs unnoticed. I fhall, however, give you a general idea of their conftruction, and you may purfue the fubject when you have more leifure.

Loli-um. The natural characters of Graffes are: Stem, Culm, or Straw, ftraight,

fim-

fimple, fiftular and jointed: *Calyx*, a hufk of two valves: *Corolla*, if it may be fo called, a dry, fkinny hufk, alfo of two valves: *Stamina* three: *Piftilla* two. Seeds, fingle, pointed at each end: Leaves, one at each joint, entire, narrow, tapering to a point. But thefe characters are not invariable, as you will fee in this fpecimen in my hand, which when I tell you its generic name, you will recollect is mentioned by Virgil more than once. It is the *Lolium temulentum*, fo called by Linnæus from the inebriating quality of its feed when malted with barley brewed.

In the Georgics you remember

——— *interque nitentia culta*
Infelix Lolium, et fteriles dominatur avenæ.

And, in the 5th Eclogue, he repeats the laft line verbatim. Whether he meant this particular fpecies I know not. It is called, in Englifh, White Darnel. If you examine it minutely you will find, that it differs from the general character of Graffes, in its *calyx* being a hufk or glume, of one leaf.

The fpecific character of this Darnel is:

Culm

Culm from two to three feet high: Spike bearded, flat, near a foot in length.

Virgil's *avena* in the verse above quoted, was probably the *Avena strigosa* of Schreber, which Dr. Withering calls Scrannel grafs.

Onopordum. The magnificent plant, with purple flowers, growing on that dry bank, demands your notice on account of its stately appearance; but more especially because of its singularity. It is the only species, in this kingdom, of the genus to which it belongs. We call it a Thistle; but that appellation comprehends several distinct *genera* in the modern system of botany. Our excellent botanist Ray, considered it as a *Carduus*, to which family it seems naturally to belong. Linnæus, after Haller, calls it *Onopordum*, with the specific name *acanthium*. It is our Cotton-thistle, so called from the grey down that gives it this whitish appearance. It is easily distinguished by its superior substance and height; its decurrent leaves, or wings, on the stem and branches, and by its very large bottom

tom leaves. But its effential generic
character is, that the *receptaculum*,
refembles a honey-comb, except that
the cells are quadrangular, and the
fcales of the calyx ftand open, and
are fharp pointed. The *receptaculum*
and the young fhoots peeled and
boiled may be eaten like artichokes.

That Thiftle about two feet high, *Car-*
with a purple flower, whofe decurrent *duus.*
leaves terminate in a long fharp fpine,
is the Spear-thiftle. It is the *Carduus
lanceolatus of Linnæus.* By this fpear
you will eafily diftinguifh it. The effential character of the *genus Carduus*
is: *Calyx* oval, imbricated, with fpinous
fcales: *Receptaculum* hairy.

That other plant with pale purple *Serra-*
fmall flowers, which you would na- *tula.*
turally call a thiftle, is according to
Linnæus, not a *Carduus,* but a *Serratula.* It differs from a *Carduus,* in
the *receptaculum* being fub-cylindri-
cal, and not fpinous. It is the *Serratula arvenfis;* in Englifh, Corn-faw-
wort,

wort, or Way-thiftle. Its flowers, which have an agreeable fmell, you obferve, grow in a kind of loofe umbel, on long peduncles, and that the entire plant is of a pale green. This is probably the Thiftle which Virgil reprobates in the following lines,

——fegnifque horreret in arvis
Carduus.

It is indeed the moft prolific, and difficult to eradicate, of any pernicious weed that infefts our corn-fields. It is impoffible to extract it with breaking every fibre of the root, which Curtis thus defcribes—*Radix perennis, teres, craffitie fere digiti minimi, fordide albida, profunde defcendens, repens, undique longiffime fe protendens.* Diffatisfied with Linnæus's arrangement of this plant, he reftores it to the *genus* Carduus, to which it naturally belongs. He gives it the Englifh name of Curfed Thiftle, "to awaken," as he fays, " the attention of the agriculturift, to its nature and pernicious effects."

We muft not quit this family—I fay family; for though arbitrary fyftems may change their names, their natural affinity
will

will remain—without taking notice of the moft beautiful among them. I mean that Thiftle whofe leaves are variegated with irregular broad white veins. It is the *Carduus marianus* or Milk Thiftle, or Lady's Thiftle. The old German Botanifts called it *Carduus Mariæ* — that is, of the *Virgin* Mary: fo our old black-letter Botanifts call it *Our Lady's Thiftle.* As the Galaxy, or Milky-way, in the Heavens was caufed by the overflowing milk of a Goddefs, fo the milk veins on this Carduus, were the effect of a fimilar redundancy in the breaft of the Virgin Mary, according to the fabulous mythology of the ancient Catholics. Thefe white veins fufficiently diftinguifh this fpecies; but fometimes they are wanting: in that cafe, you muft attend to the large thorns, befet with a few fmall ones, which guard the *calyx*. You may likewife obferve, that there is a fingle head on the top of each branch; that there is no leaf near it, and that the leaves embrace the ftem.

I fuppofe you are now fo much a botanift, that it is almoft unneceffary to tell you that thefe Thiftles are of the Clafs and Or-

U

der

der *Syngenesia Polygamia æqualis:* the *flosculi,* you observe, are all turbular and hermaphrodite.

Adieu.

LETTER XXXII.

YOUR objection to this Sexual Syſtem of Linnæus, carries more weight upon reflection, than might, at firſt, be ſuppoſed. The lady who aſked the queſtion, "whether women may be inſtructed in the modern Syſtem of Botany, conſiſtently with female delicacy?"—was accuſed of ridiculous prudery; neverthelefs, if ſhe had propoſed the queſtion to me, I ſhould certainly have anſwered — "They cannot."

The late Dr. Hope, Profeſſor of Botany at Edinburgh, was naturally a very modeſt man. I have frequently ſeen him embarraſſed under the neceſſity of explaining the analogy between the parts of generation in plants and animals, to an audience of young pupils. How much greater would have been his embarraſſment, if his pupils had been females! — It is true, the terms are Latin, or of Latin derivation; and it is alſo true, that there is nothing indecent in their literal meaning; but, unleſs we explain their analogy, the Sexual Syſtem does not appear.

The

·The idea of male and female plants, is of very ancient date. The penetrating, the inquisitive genius of Linnæus, purfued the idea, faw its want of precifion, difcovered the fexual diftinctions, and made them the foundation of a beautiful philofophical hypothefis. But this hypothefis might have been confined to Philofophy. The analogy between the parts, and the propagation, of plants and animals, was of no ufe in a practical fyftem of Botany. Five *ftamina* and one *piftillum* would fufficiently afcertain the Clafs and Order *Pentandria Monogynia*, which might with great eafe have been otherwife denominated, fo as to have no reference to fex.

In an age lefs refined than the prefent, thefe objections were invalid. Poffibly we may not be more virtuous than our progenitors; but doubtlefs we are more delicate. The *double entendres* in the comedies of the laft age, with which the then audience were fo much delighted, would now be received with difguft: and, what is very remarkable, though we are, by no means, efteemed the moft polifhed nation, we are certainly the moft delicate. Some years ago, I was prefent, on a Sunday evening, at the repre-

fentation

fentation of a French comic Opera, at Brux-
elles. One of the fongs was at leaft *treble
entendre*, and in another, (a *duetto* between a
man and woman) he made feveral attempts
to put his hands in the girl's bofom. I believe, this would hardly have been fuffered
at Bartholomew-fair.

The French have the reputation of a
highly polifhed people. This reputation
may be juft: neverthelefs they are indelicate; fo extremely indelicate, that, paradoxi-
cal as it may feem, even their modeft women are difguftingly immodeft. A modeft
Englifhwoman is the moft modeft woman
in the world. If the ftage be the juft criterion of the manners of a nation, we are,
at this time, fuperior in point of public
chaftity.

The fweet fmell that you perceive in *Tilia.*
this avenue proceeds from thefe tall
trees, which are now in bloom. They
are the *Tilia europæa*, Lime-trees, of the
Clafs and Order *Polyandria Monadelphia:* you will accordingly find, in the
flower, many *ftamina* and one *piftillum*.
The *corolla* is pentapetalous and the
calyx quinquepartite. The fpecies is

dif-

diftinguifhed by its want of a nectarium, and by the fingular pale-green ftrap, called a *bractea*, annexed to the pedunculus, that fupports an umbel of from three to feven radii, with one flower at the extremity of each. The leaves, you fee, are heart-fhaped and finely ferrated. Virgil celebrates this tree for the lightnefs of the wood.

———*Tilia ante juga lævis.*

Pafti-naca.
That tall umbelliferous plant, which grows fo profufely on the border of this field, I fee, attracts your particular notice. You have hitherto feen no plant of this ftructure whofe flowers were yellow; and that circumftance is alone fufficient to inform me that it is the *Paftinaca fylveftris*, or Wild Parfnip. It has no *involucrum* either general or partial. Its petals are involuted and entire, and its leaves are fimply pinnated. The general umbel confifts of about ten radii, and the partial of as many more. You will find it in the Clafs and Order *Pentandria Digynia.*

Obferve

Obſerve that plant of an umbelli- *Achillea.*
ferous appearance, whoſe innumerable ſmall flowers are of a beautiful
red-purple: they are generally white.
It is of the Claſs and Order *Syngeneſia Polygamia ſuperflua:* you will accordingly find that the *floſculi* in the
diſk contain *ſtamina* and *piſtilla*; and
thoſe of the radius, which are about
five in number, *piſtilla* only. It is
the *Achillea millefolium*; in Engliſh,
Yarrow. It is called *millefolium*, from
the numerous diviſion of its leaves.
There is an engraving of this plant
in the *Flora Londinenſis*, in which
the flower is drawn with too little
attention to perſpective.

That noble plant, among the corn, *Centau-*
with beautiful purple flowers on the *rea.*
top of imbricated black-green globes,
is of the ſame genus, and conſequently of the ſame Claſs and Order,
with the *Centaurea cyanus* or Blue-
bottle, which you examined laſt
month: accordingly, you will find,
that the exterior *floſculi* have no *piſtillum*; that they are tubular, larger

U 4

than

than thofe of the difk, and irregu-
larly divided. It is the *Centaurea fca-
biofa*, Great Knapweed or Matfellon.
The flowers, you obferve, are fingle
and raifed on long naked ftalks. The
fcales of the calyx are edged with a
brown fringe; but, what particularly
diftinguifhes the fpecies, is the pinnatifid leaves. The *Centaurea nigra*,
which generally grows in meadows,
refembles this plant; but it has no
neutral *flofculi*, its leaves are lance-
fhaped, and the flowers lefs.

*Sca-
biofa.* You fee, among the corn, a very tall,
flender, plant, with long peduncles,
each fupporting a fingle pale-purple
flower. The ftem meafures at leaft
four feet and a half. I take particular
notice of it, becaufe its natural fize is
about a third of that height. If you
now examine the flower, you will find,
that it confifts of a number of fmall
flofculi: You conclude, therefore, without hefitation, that you are to look for
it in the Clafs *Syngenefia*. You are
miftaken. Nature would fo have claffed
it; but Art tyrannically tears it from

its

its relations. It wants the eſſential characteriſtic of the Claſs *Syngeneſia:* its *ſtamina* are not united. If you examine any of the *floſculi,* you will find, that they contain four *ſtamina* and one *piſtillum:* therefore you muſt turn to the Claſs *Tetrandria,* and Order, *Monogynia. Scabioſa,* the ſecond plant in this Claſs, is the *genus,* and *arvenſis* the ſpecies. The *genus* is determined by the common *calyx* conſiſting of many leaves, and the proper *calyx* being double and above the germin. The ſpecific character is — *corolla* quadrifid, radiant; leaves oppoſite; pinnatifid, ending in a lance; ſtem cylindrical and rough. You will find a good engraving of this plant in the *Flora Londinenſis,* except that it appears rather dwarfiſh.

Among that wheat you ſee a bright purple flower, which for ſimple elegance is not ſurpaſſed by any of the exotics in our gardens, green-houſes, or hot-houſes: but we eſtimate things, not by their beauty, but by their ſcarcity; elſe who would exchange ten guineas for Cromwell's halfpenny? *Agroſtemma.*

ny? This plant is too common for general admiration. It is eafily diftinguifhed by the colour of its five obcordate petals, and by the extreme length of the fegments of its monophyllous *calyx*. You will find it to be of the Clafs and Order *Decandria Pentagynia*, and of the *genus* Agroftemma, of which four *fpecies* have been difcovered in different parts of the world; but this, our Cockle, to which Linnæus has given the trivial, or fpecific, name of *githago*, is the only one indigenous in this kingdom. There is an excellent engraving of it in the *Flora Londinenfis*.

Dau-
cus. There is an umbelliferous plant in bloom, the name of which, from the defcription of modern Botanifts, it is impoffible, in its prefent ftate, to difcover; becaufe both the generic and fpecific defcriptions, given by Linnæus, depend principally on the feeds, which are not yet formed; but, by applying the root to your nofe, you will immediately tell me, it is a Carrot. It is indeed the *Daucus carota*, the Wild Carrot,

rot, and differs only from that which is cultivated in our gardens, in the colour and fubftance of its root, which is the effect of culture. You will find, on examination, that it is of the Clafs and Order, *Pentandria Digynia.* Linnæus's generic charaƈter is: *Corollæ fubradiatæ, omnes hermaphroditæ. Fruƈtus pilis hifpidis:* and his fpecific diftinƈtion, *Seminibus hifpidis, petiolis fubtus nervofis.* To this may be added, from Relhan, that the ftem is fulcated and alfo hifpid; that the general *involucrum* confifts of many pinnatifid leaves; that the umbels have 40 radii, and the *umbellulæ* 30.

I fee a beautiful blue flower in the border of this corn-field, which it would have been criminal to overlook, as it is, in its wild ftate, peculiar to this county. You are well acquainted with it as a garden flower. It is the garden Larkfpur, but growing wild in great abundance, and variety of colour, in almoft every part of the extenfive fields fouth of Cambridge. The Linnæan name is *Delphinium confolida*, of the Clafs and Order Polyandria Trigynia.

If

*Dip-
facus.*   If you had ever lived in any part of the kingdom where woollen cloth is manufactured, you would immediately have recognized that upright plant with large oval heads, growing, in numbers, by the fide of this ditch. It is the *Dipfacus fylveftris*, the Wild Teafel, of the Clafs and Order *Tetrandria Monogynia*. It is, indeed, not the fpecies ufed in the woollen manufactory; but there is fo little difference between this and the *fullonum*, that Linnæus confidered the latter as a variety of the *fylveftris:* neverthelefs there is certainly a fpecific diftinction. In the *D. fullonum*, the *paleæ* of the *receptaculum* are hooked downwards: in the *D. fylveftris*, they are ftraight. In the *D. fullonum*, the leaves of the *involucrum* are fhort and horizontal: in the *fylveftris*, they are long, and, as you fee, encircle the head. The generic character is — Calyx *communis* polyphyllus; *proprius* fuperus. *Receptaculum* paleaceum.

The ufe of the Teafel in the manufactory of woollen cloth, is to lay the pile all one way, before it is put in the hot prefs. For
this

this purpose about a score of the heads of the Teasel are fixed in a wooden frame, or crofs, and bound together by a small cord. This instrument is drawn along the wet cloth lengthwise, forcibly and repeatedly, the piece being suspended over a perch, and gradually drawn from one end to the other, till the whole has undergone this discipline.

The Cloth-dreffers, in the North of England, sometimes shut themselves up, for the clandestine purpose of using, instead of these legal Teasels, *Cards* with wire teeth, similar to those which are used for carding wool. These *Cards* were supposed to injure the substance of the cloth, an act of Parliament was therefore obtained to prohibit their use; but they are more durable and consequently less expensive. Probably we learnt this application of the Teasel from the Germans, who have given it a name expressive of its use. They call it *Kartendistel*, that is, Card-thistle.

Vale.

L E T-

LETTER XXXIII.

JULY.

I PROMISED you, in a former letter, an excurfion to the celebrated Chalk-pit Clofe at Cherry Hinton: celebrated, becaufe it contains a great variety of plants; becaufe it was frequently vifited by Ray, the father of Englifh Botanifts; and becaufe my worthy friend Relhan, on this fpot, recovered the long loft *Athamanta libanotis:* I fay *recovered*, becaufe Dr. Withering in the firft volume of his *Botanical Arrangement* miftakes the fact, in faying that Mr. Relhan firft difcovered this plant in Britain. Mr. Relhan never pretended to any fuch original difcovery, well knowing that Ray had found it on Gog-magog hills; but, no Botanift, fince Ray's time, before Mr. Relhan, had been able to find it. He claims only the merit of difcovering a plant, which, for many years, had been totally loft. This explanation is the more neceffary, becaufe Dr. Withering, in the firft part of his third volume, lately publifhed, deviates ftill farther from the truth, in quoting the autho-

rity

rity of Mr. Woodward. But you will not, to day, have the fatisfaction of feeing this fcarce plant, as it does not flower till Auguft.

The Chalk-pit Clofe will afford us fufficient matter for this day's amufement; we fhall therefore not begin till we come upon the field of action: and, to fatisfy your curiofity as to the number of plants now in bloom within the fmall compafs of this Chalk-pit Clofe, the beft way will be to collect them in your tin-box, and we will afterwards fit down and examine them.

Well — now open your budget.

No. 1. It is the *Carduus acaulis*, Dwarf Thiftle. You will find it, in *Carduus acaulis.* your Synopfis, the tenth fpecies of this *genus* in the Clafs and Order *Syngenefia, Polygamia æqualis.* Its having no ftem is a fufficient diftinction. Sometimes it is found with a ftem an inch or more in length. This fpecimen has no ftem at all.

No. 2. *Verbena officinalis*, Vervain. *Verbena.* You will find it the firft *genus* in the

Clafs

Clafs and Order *Didynamia Gymnofper-mia*; and there can be no doubt of the *fpecies*, as there is but one. The flower, you obferve, is fo very minute, that to convince yourfelf of its Clafs and Order you muft have recourfe to your glafs; and alfo of its *genus*, which depends on the *calyx* being monophyllous, with one of its five teeth truncated, and on its having four feeds. You will know the *fpecies*, by the fpikes being very long with a few reddifh pale blue flowers near the extremity, by its having a fingle ftem, and the leaves oppofite and with nu-merous clefts.

It feems very extraordinary that this in-fignificant plant fhould have acquired fo much importance in ancient times. Pliny tells us it was carried by Embaffadors when they were fent to demand fatisfaction for depredations, and that he who carried the plant was called *Verbenarius*. He alfo in-forms us that is was ufed for fweeping the table of Jupiter—*His Jovis menfa verritur, domus pergantur luftranturque.*

From Livy we learn that the plant Ver-bena was ufed in the ceremony when the

league

league was ratified between Tullius Hofti-
lius, third King of the Romans, and the
Albans.   It was alfo ufed in incantations.

Effer aquam et molli cinge hæc altaria vitta;
Verbenafque adole pingues et mafcula thura.

This Verbena *pinguis* cannot poffibly be
the plant we call Vervain; unlefs, in compaffion to the poverty of the Latin language,
we tranflate it frefh, *full of juice.*   I recollect another paffage in Virgil, as little applicable to our Vervain.   In the fourth book
of the Georgics, fpeaking of the old Cory-
cian's garden,

Hic rarum tamen in dumis olus, albaque circum
Lilia, verbenafque premens, vefcumque papaver,
Regum æquabat opes animis.

So that this contented old man thought
himfelf as rich as a King, with a few ftrag-
gling cabbages, furrounded by lilies, vervain
and poppies; the laft of which feems to have
made part of his food, unlefs we tranflate
vefcum *meager,* a fenfe in which, I think it
is fometimes ufed; but as to this border of
Vervain, if it be our plant, it could neither
be for ufe nor ornament.   Probably fuper-

X

ftition

ſtition introduced it into the gardens of the ancients. On the ſame foundation a quack in this kingdom, a few years ago, publiſhed a pamphlet on the infallibity of the root of Vervain, worn round the neck, for the cure of the King's Evil. It was thought, by the ancient phyſicians, to poſſeſs great medical virtues. It is juſt as uſeful in Medicine, as in the art of Incantation.

Convol-
vulus. No. 3. *Convolvulus arvenſis*, Small Bindweed: *Pentandria Monogynia.* The corolla, you obſerve, is campanulate and plaited, and the piſtillum has a double *ſtigma.* The ſtems are generally numerous, weak and trailing. The leaves are ſhaped like the head of an arrow, with three acute points: In the *Convolvulus ſepium,* Great Bindweed, the two poſterior angles of the leaf are truncated. The flowers are white, as in this ſpecimen, or pale pink.

No. 4. *Anthyllis vulneraria,* Ladies-finger. This is an old acquaintance: you have examined it laſt month.

No. 5.

No. 5. *Verbafcum thapfus.* Great *Verbaf-*
Mullen: *Pentandria Monogynia.* The *cum.*
corolla has a very fhort tube, is fixed
below the germen, and has 5 obtufe
fegments. . The fpecies you will diftinguifh by its decurrent leaves; its
fix-feet fimple ftem, terminated by a
long clofe fpike of yellow flower, and
by the greenifh-white flannelly appearance and feel of the entire plant.

No. 6. *Campanula glomerata:* Can- *Campa-*
terbury-bells. The corolla you ob- *nula.*
ferve is regular, of one petal and below the germen: it is bell-fafhioned,
and clofed at the bottom by 5 valves
which fupport the ftamina. The
ftigma is trifid: thefe particulars conftitute it a Campanula, and the fpecies is characterized, by the ftem being erect, angular, fimple; and the
flowers, generally blue, growing three
together in the alæ of the leaves. Relhan obferves that the height of the
ftem varies from three feet to three
inches.

 No. 7.

No. 7. *Liguſtrum vulgare:* Privet. This you ſaw laſt month.

Ru-
bus. No. 8. I need not tell you, that this is the common Bramble, or Blackberry. It is the Rubus of Linnæus and of all former ſyſtematic Botaniſts. The Claſs and Order are *Icoſandria Polygynia.* The generic character is perfectly diſtinct and obvious, viz. *Calyx* quinquefid: *Petala* five: Berry compoſed of many ſmall ones with a ſingle ſeed in each. Linnæus enumerates no leſs than twenty ſpecies of this *genus,* of which no more than five are natives of Britain, and but two of Cambridgeſhire, namely, the *Cæſius,* Small Bramble or Dewberry, and this *Fruticous* or Common Bramble. It is diſtinguiſhed by its long, trailing, ſpinous, ſtem; by its 3 or 5-fingered leaves, white flowers and black fruit.

Carduus
eriopho-
rus. No. 9. *Carduus eriphorus.* Woolly-headed Thiſtle. This Thiſtle may be immediately diſtinguiſhed by the ſingularity of its leaves which exactly

actly refemble a *Cheveau de Frize,*
their fegments pointing four different ways, and terminated by a fharp
thorn, which is the only thorn upon
them. The lowermoft of thefe leaves
are frequently eighteen or twenty
inches in length.

No. 10. *Papaver rhoeas,* which you are
already acquainted with.

No. 11. Is the little plant *Euphra-* Euphra-
fia officinalis. It frequently grows *fia.*
much higher than this fpecimen,
the ftem of which is not above four
inches. You will find it in the Clafs
and Order *Didynamia, Angcofpermia.*
The *calyx,* you obferve, is of one
leaf, cylindrical, quadrifid, the fegments not quite equal. Now take
your glafs and you will difcover, that
the *antheræ* are purple, with each
two lobes with a fpine at the bafe.
The *corolla* is ringent. Such is the
genus Euphrafia, of which there are,
in all, feven *fpecies.* We have in this
kingdom but two of them. This
which you have gathered, is called

X 3

fimply

simply Eyebright; the other, *E. odon-tites*, or Red Eyebright. As the firſt was to cure diſeaſes of the eyes, ſo the latter, as I ſuppoſe from the ſpecific name, was deemed a remedy for thoſe of the teeth. They are eaſily diſtinguiſhed. Of the *officinalis* the flowers are generally white or purpliſh; the ſtalk purple and about 5 or 6 inches long; the leaves oval in pairs with very ſharp teeth. Of the *odontites*, the flowers are fleſhcolour, in lateral ſpikes; the ſtem green, much branched, ten or twelve inches long; the leaves are lance-ſhaped, thinly indented and moſt of them purple.

Orchis, pyrami-dalis. No. 12. I ſhould imagine, that the moment you beheld this beautiful purple flower, you were ſtruck with a family reſemblance to a plant which you examined two months ago. It is indeed of the ſame genus with the *Orchis morio*, which we met with near Impington, in the month of May. This is called *Orchis pyramidalis*, Pyramidal Orchis, which appellation,

pellation, alluding to the ſhape of the ſpike, is almoſt ſufficient to diſtinguiſh it from any other *ſpecies*; but if you add, that the horn is remarkably long; that the ſtem is ten or twelve inches in length, and entirely inveloped by its leaves, you will be in no danger of miſtaking it for any other Orchis.

No. 13. *Plantago major.* Great Plantain. Of the Claſs and Order *Tetrandria Monogynia.* Theſe very minute flowers are an inſuperable objection to the Linnæan ſyſtem. If, however, the uſe of a ſyſtematic arrangement of plants be only to trace them to their *generic* and ſpecific names, the *habitus* of the Plantains is ſo obviouſly diſtinct, that we may leave ſyſtem out of the queſtion. This *ſpecies* is known by the leaves being broader, ſlightly indented, and not downy, and by the antheræ being purple, and the ſpike longer than in *Plantago media*, from which in appearance it differs very little.

No. 14. That is the *Hedyſarum onobrychis,* which

which you faw in our laft excurfion to the hills.

Hyperi-cum. No. 15. *Hypericum perforatum*, Common St. John's-wort; of the Clafs and Order *Polyadelphia Polyandria:* you perceive, accordingly, that the numerous ftamina are united at the bottom in three *fafciculi*, not very diftinctly indeed, but fufficiently obvious to bring the plant within the pale of this Clafs. Linnæus's character of this genus is—*Calyx quinquepartitus: Petala quinque: Filamenta multa, in quinque phalanges bafi connata: Capfula fubrotunda*—But, in this plant, there are only three phalanxes of *ftamina:* No matter. The character agrees with moft of the *fpecies*, of which there are no lefs than 42. Eight of thefe have been found in this kingdom, two of which are wanting in Cambridgefhire. This *Hypericum perforatum* is diftinguifhed by its being a ftraight flender plant, about two feet high; its upper branches terminated by yellow flower, with 3 divaricating *ftyli* in the

centre

centre of each; a black fpot on the antheræ, and the leaves apparently perforated. Hypericum is the only *genus* of the Clafs, that is a native of Britain.

No. 16. *Carduus crifpus*, or Curled Thiftle. This plant has caufed fome confufion among our Englifh Bota‑ nifts. Hudfon's *C. crifpus* is the *acanthoides* of Linnæus, and his acan‑ thoides, the *crifpus* of that author. Dr. Withering rejects the *crifpus* of Linnæus, and fubftitutes a new fpe‑ cies which he calls *C. inclinans.* Old Bauhinus very properly calls it *Cardu‑ us fpinofiffimus anguftifolius vulgaris.* It is indeed prickly all over. It refem‑ bles moft the *C. nutans*, Mufk Thiftle; but differs in the decurrent leaves covering the entire ftem: it is alfo faid to be rather more ftiffnecked than the *nutans.* I have not found it fo. But there is a peculiarity ob‑ fervable in this *crifpus*, which, I be‑ lieve, no writer has taken notice of. It is fo delicately fenfible of the night air, that towards evening it con‑
ftantly

Carduus crifpus.

ftantly turns its face from the wind, and then fhews its naked white neck behind, like that of a nodding Mandarine on the chimney-piece. Four fpecies of Thiftles you will fee, in great abundance, in the road to Trumpington, viz. The *Onopordum acanthium*, or Cotton Thiftle; *Carduus lanceolatus*, or Spear Thiftle; *Serratula arvenfis*, or Curfed Thiftle; and the *Carduus crifpus*, or Curled Thiftle. The firft you diftinguifh immediately by its mealy appearance. The fecond by its *dark*; the third by its light green colour, and the laft by a fhade between the two.

No. 17. This is the *Daucus carota.*

No. 18. And this, *Paftinaca fylveftris*, both which we have before examined. Thefe are all you have gathered. You have overlooked a few; but I fuppofe your box would hold no more.

Vale.

L E T-

LETTER XXXIV.

August.

THIS morning we shall pay a second visit to the Chalk-pit Close, for the particular purpose of shewing you the *Athamanta libanotis*. When I first beheld this rare plant in company with my friend Relhan, he insisted on my taking off my hat; a ceremony, which, he told me, the celebrated author of the *Flora Anglica*, had most reverendly observed. You will be surprised to find, that there is nothing extraordinary in its appearance: its sole merit lies in its scarcity.—Here it is. You have seen many common umbelliferous plants, of much the same appearance. Like the rest, it is of the Class and Order, *Pentandria Digynia.*

The generic character of the plant is — *Fructus ovato-oblongus, striatus. Petala inflexa, emarginata;* and the specific character —*foliis bipinnatis planis, umbella hemispherica, seminibus hirsutis:* so that both the generic and specific characters depend upon the seed.

Atha-manta.

feed. However, if you attend to a few obvious particulars, which I ſhall point out, you will eaſily recogniſe the plant, if you ſhould ever meet with it in any other part of the kingdom. Firſt, you obſerve, it is an umbelliferous plant, neither tall nor very ſtout; that the umbel conſiſting of many radii has a conſiderable convexity, and that it is rather grey than white. The ſtem, you ſee, is angular and unequally furrowed. The leaves are bipinnated ſomewhat reſembling thoſe of parſley, except that the *pinnæ* are ſeſſile, and that the baſe of every leaf ſheaths either the ſtem or ſtalk which ſupports the umbel. To theſe obſervations you may add, that the root is ſhaped like a carrot, though not ſo regularly ſtraight; that it is acrid but ſomewhat aromatic, and that it is bearded or fringed at the top, with a tuft of leaves like hair—*vertice barbato*, in the language of Linnæus. There is a good engraving of this plant in Relhan. The Engliſh name is, Mountain Stone-parſley, given it, I ſuppoſe, by Ray,

who

who firft found it on Gog-magog
Hills.

Well—You have now had the fatisfaction of *culling a fimple*, which very few Botanifts in this kingdom have ever feen.

There ftands another plant of the *Pimpi-*
fame umbelliferous family. It is the *nella.*
Pimpinella magna, Burnet Saxifrage.
It firft blooms in July; fo that.you
muft have overlooked it when we
were laft here. You fee, it has neither general nor partial involucrum;
the firft confifts of about 14 *radii*,
and the latter from 10 to 18, according to Relhan. I have generally
found them nearly equal. The ftem
is furrowed and 2 to 3 feet high.
The leaves are lobed, ferrated, oily,
and broader than they are long, but
grow narrow and almoft entire as
they afcend.—Let us now continue
our walk.

If I miftake not, that diffufe plant, *The-*
with long crooked ftems partly trail-*fium.*
ing, and terminated by loofe fpikes of
fmall white flowers, is the *Thefium lino-*
phyllum,

phyllum, which Relhan has thought de-
ferving a plate in his *Flora*; for which
reafon you may conclude it not very
common. It is of the Clafs and Order
Pentandria Monogynia. Its Englifh name
is Baftard Toadflax. – The calyx is of
one leaf, into which the *ftamina* are in-
ferted. The feed is fingle. The leaves
are numerous, long and narrow. There
are 17 *fpecies* of this *genus*, of which this
is the only indigenous in England. We
might have feen it in flower above a
month ago.

Ophrys. That plant with a fingle ftem
about feven inches high with a fpike
of greenifh white flowers, running
fpirally to the top, is nearly allied
to the Orchis family; and it was fo
called by Ray and other Botanifts.
Its prefent generic and fpecific ap-
pellations are *Ophrys fpiralis*. Its Clafs
and Order are, *Gynandria Diandria*.
It differs from the Orchis only in
the form of the *nectarium*, which, in
the Ophrys, is flightly carinated underneath. If you take up the root,
you will find feveral long bulbs,
which,

which, with the spiral difposition of the flowers, fufficiently afcertain the *fpecies.* The Englifh name is Tripple Ladies-traces. There are no lefs than 28 *fpecies* of this *genus,* eleven of which are natives of this kingdom.

That plant, about a foot high, with feveral branched ftems, termi-nated by bunches of blue cup-fafhi-oned flowers, is of a very irregular *genus,* which, therefore, folicits your attention. It is a *Gentiana,* of which Linnæus enumerates 39 *fpecies:* of thefe, five only are natives of this ifland. They are according to Lin-næus, of the Clafs and Order *Pentandria Digynia*; but of thefe five, two properly belong to the Clafs *Tetrandria,* where you will find them in the *Synopfis*; and where they cer-tainly ought to be. If the prime dif-tinction, that of Clafs, be not abfo-lute, the fyftem is of no ufe to a young Botanift. This plant, how-ever, which you have gathered, has five *ftamina.* It is the *Gentiana amarella,* Autumnal Gentian, or Felwort.

The

The generic character is: *Corolla* monopetalous; *capsula* bivalve unilocular; *receptaculum* two, longitudinal. The Linnæan character of the *species* is *corollis quinquefidis hypocrateriformibus, fauce barbatis.* But, says Relhan, *numerus segmentorum calycis et corollæ, nil valet:* so that you must depend principally on this beard, which, by the bye, is inside the mouth. The leaves, you observe, are lance-shaped. Pliny says the plant *Gentian* was so called from Gentius, King of Illyria. I do not remember the name of any other King of this country. There is indeed a Duke of Illyria, with whom I have the pleasure to be well acquainted. His name is Orsino. You remember him in *The Twelfth Night.* Sir Thomas Hanmer, in *The Winter's Tale,* alters the kingdom of Polixenes from Bohemia to Bithynia, on a supposition that it was a blunder of some transcriber; because he thinks it impossible that Shakespeare should have been so ignorant, as not to know, that Bohemia was an inland country; whereas the kingdom
which

which Polixenes governed, was, evidently, maritime. As to Shakespeare's geographical ignorance, there are other instances of it, equally flagrant. In *The Two Gentlemen of Verona*, he makes one of them *embark* at Verona for Milan, and the servants talk of saving the tide. Would Shakespeare have done this, if he had known that these are both inland cities; that they have no communication whatever by water, and that there is no tide in the Mediterranean. Sir Thomas Hanmer was certainly right in blotting out the absurd Bohemia; but Illyria would have been a better substitute than Bithynia, which Bithynia was situated on the black Sea, opposite to the present Constantinople. This Bithynia appears, from a line in Claudian, to have been very anciently called Thrace.

Thyni Thraces erant, quæ nunc Bithynia fertur.

Probably it was peopled by a colony of Thracians crossing the Bosphorus, and therefore called *Thracia Asiatica.* Now it is very improbable that Antigonus, who embarked

Y

from

from Sicily for no other purpofe than to expofe the infant, fhould make a long voyage, through the Archipelago to the Black Sea. But Illyria bordered on the Adriatic, at a moderate diftance from Sicily. Thefe geographical truths are indifpenfably neceffary in every reprefentation, though fabulous. The majority of an Englifh audience may bear an embarkation from Verona; but what would an Italian fay, who might be prefent at the reprefentation? Would he not naturally whifper to his companion — " This great Shakefpeare of the Englifh, was an ignorant blockhead." I have as fincere a veneration for the memory of Shakefpeare, and feel his beauties as exquifitely as any of his moft enthufiaftic commentators; but no veneration for authentic abfurdities fhould prevent me from obliterating his palpable miftakes.

If you can bear the fudden tranfition from his Illyrian Majefty to a heap of rubbifh — from a King to a dunghill — this wafte will afford you fome inftruction, and, confequently, I prefume, fome pleafure. Pleafure is the object of purfuit of all mankind; but, notwithftanding its feeming reality, from its appearing in a different fhape

to

to almoſt every individual, one would be apt to ſuppoſe it a phantom, an *ignis fatuus.* You are yet a ſtripling. You have ſcarce looked into manhood; it cannot therefore be expected that you have thought much about the matter. At your age, ſenſual pleaſures are powerfully attractive; but powerful as they are, you cannot avoid reflecting, that you have them in common with the brute creation; it were therefore too degrading to human nature to ſuppoſe, that ſenſual pleaſure is its *ſummum bonum;* that, with faculties ſo infinitely ſuperior to the animal world, man was created incapable of pleaſures above thoſe enjoyed by other animals, and probably by them in a higher degree.

From theſe reflections, you are naturally induced to direct your attention towards the pleaſures of the mind, as moſt congenial to your rank in the creation; and I will venture to aſſure you, that nothing will afford you ſo much pleaſure as the purſuit of knowledge. The celebrated Dr. Prieſtley, in a preface to one of his philoſophical publications, very pleaſingly and ingeniouſly ſuppoſes, that he ſhall carry his multifarious acquirements to the next world, and, very

ra-

rationally, confiders his infatiable thirft of knowledge, as a powerful argument in proof of a future ftate.

Chenopo-
dium.   You obferve a plant, about a foot in height, near that dunghill; with fhort, fpread, flat bunches of green flowers, and leaves fomewhat refembling, in fhape, the foot of a goofe, and not very unlike the leaves of a nettle. It is the *Chenopodium murale*, Goofe-foot or Sowbane, of the Clafs and Order *Pentandria Digynia.* The *calyx* is pentaphyllous and pentagonous: *corolla* it has none. Its leaves are gloffy, and the whole plant has a difagreeable fmell. By thefe circumftances you will diftinguifh it from the other fpecies of which there are twelve in this kingdom, and twenty in all. The *genus* is eafily known by the green flowers, the goofe-foot leaves, and their growth near dunghills and among rubbifh.
Our homeward rout now lies along the verdant banks of this rivulet

——— *varios hic flumina circum*
Fundit humus flores.

If

If you pull one of thofe bunches of fmall cream coloured flowers, you will find they have a ftrong kernel odor. They refemble apparently the flower of the common Elder; but you will find them of the Clafs and Order, *Icofandria Pentagynia*. It is the *Spiræa ulmaria*, Meadow-fweet. You cannot miftake the *genus*, becaufe there are, in this kingdom, but two of this Clafs and Order, one of which is the Wild Pear-tree. There are alfo but two fpecies of the *Spiræa*. The other is the *S. filipendula*, Dropwort: it is a much lefs plant, and is particularly diftinguifhed by the oblong glands at the extremity of the fibres of its root.

That plant with purplifh red flowers, of four obcordate petals, with leaves refembling thofe of the Willow, is the *Epilobium hirfutum*, Large-flowered Willow-herb, or Codlings and Cream, fo called from its fmell, which has been fuppofed to refemble the fmell of apples and cream. You will find it to be of the Clafs and Order *Octandria Monogynia*. The genus is characterized by its five-leaved *calyx*, four petals, oblong

Spiræa.

cap-

capsula, and downy feed; and you will diftinguifh the fpecies by the flower being much larger than that of any other *Spiræa*, and by its ftem and leaves being hairy.

Car-duus. On the oppofite fide of the rivulet I fee a fpecies of Thiftle which we have never yet met with. It differs fufficiently, in appearance, from the reft. Its flowers are of a deeper purple, and grow two or three together like a clufter of filberds. The calyx is clofely imbricated and fmooth. The upper leaves are few, narrow, and often curled. It is the *Carduus paluftris*, or Marfh Thiftle.

We have, I believe, examined, in our feveral perambulations, at leaft, fourfcore different plants, of various Claffes, Orders, Genera and Species: a fmall number, in proportion to all the indigenous plants of this ifland; but a number amply fufficient for a botanical foundation. In the fucceeding months, were we to continue our excurfions, we fhould meet with few plants in flower that would either add to your bo-

tanical

tanical knowledge, or call to your recollection a line in any claffical author; except the *Hedera*, which Virgil tells us, indicates a cold foil.

—————— *at fceleratam exquirere frigus*
Difficile eft: piceæ tantum, faxique nocentes
Interdum, aut hederæ pandunt vefligia nigræ.

Nigræ, I fuppofe, becaufe the berries are black. That poets were crowned with Ivy we learn from this line.

Paftores hederâ crefcentem ornate poetam.

You will not find the Ivy in bloffom till October: it is of the Clafs and Order *Pentandria Monogynia.*

You are now qualified to proceed with eafe, if you feel delighted in the purfuit: if not, you have learnt no more than, I fhould imagine, every man who has had the advantage of an Univerfity education, ought to know. But, in the Sciences, alps on alps are continually arifing before us. Happily for the Enthufiaft in knowledge, he is in no danger of weeping with the Macedonian madman, that there are no more worlds to conquer. In the Linnæan Syftem of Botany,

the

the moſt numerous Claſs of Plants, we have left entirely unnoticed, I mean the *Cryptoga-mia*. Of theſe I purpoſe to give you a general idea in my next letter, mean while,

Adieu.

LETTER XXXV.

CRYPTOGAMIA, from *κρυπτος occultus* and *γαμος nuptiæ*, you know is the twenty-fourth Claſs in the Linnæan Syſtem. You alſo know that it is ſo denominated becauſe the *modus propagandi* is concealed, either from minuteneſs, or within the fruit: in the language of Linnæus, *nuptiæ clam celebrantur*. The Orders are four, viz. *Filices, Muſci, Algæ, Fungi.*

FILICES. This Order comprehends the plants commonly known by the name of Ferns, whoſe fruĉtification is on the back-ſide of the *frondes*, or leaves. The *genera* which have been diſcovered in this king-dom are,

Equiſetum, Horſe-tail. The plants of this *genus* bear no reſemblance to Ferns: they are ſhaped rather like little Pines, from one to three feet high. They elevate their fruĉtification on the top of a naked ſpike proceeding from the root. The ſtem and leaves are com-poſed of tubes inſerted into each other

at

at the joints, which leaves ftand in whirls gradually diminifhing to the top. If you fhake a little of the duft from the fpike on a fheet of white paper, and examine it with a good glafs; you will fee it fkip, as if it were alive. There are of this genus feven fpecies, fix of which have been found in this kingdom. In the *Flora Londinenfis* you will fee a good print of the *Equifetum ar-venfe*.

Ophioglofum. Of this genus there are nine fpecies, but one of which has been found in Britain: it is the *O. vulgatum*, common Adder's Tongue. Its generic character is—*Spica articulata, difticha; articulis tranfverfim dehifcentibus.* It is a fingle, thick, oval, leaf, without rib or veins, on a foot-ftalk four inches long.

Ofmunda. Of thefe the fpike is branched, and the capfules globular. There are four fpecies in this kingdom. One of them is the *O. fpicans*, you will find it in *Curtis.* We call it Rough Spleenwort. The feeds are only on the center-leaves, which are more erect and the wings more diftinct.

Acrof-

Acrostichum. Fructifications cover the entire difk of the leaf. We have two *species* of this *genus.* They both grow out of the fiffures of rocks in Wales, &c.

Pteris aquilina. This is our only *species* of this *genus,* though there are, in different parts of the world, no lefs than 23. It is diftinguifhed from other ferns by the fructifications being in marginal lines. It is our moft common Fern, or female Fern, or Brakes, or, in Yorkfhire, Brackons. It is that fpecies commonly burnt for the afhes, which yield a large proportion of vegetable alkali. Linnæus gave it the trivial name of *aquilina,* from the fuppofed figure of the Imperial Eagle in the root when cut obliquely. Lightfoot fays, that potatoes planted on this fern never fail to produce a plentiful crop; that in Normandy the wretched inhabitants are fometimes reduced to the neceffity of mixing its roots with their bread. I hope the revolution in France, will, in its confequences, relieve them from this neceffity. It was formerly much ufed medically in obftructions of the

vifcera,

viscera, and the root is still prescribed, in powder, as an anthelmintic.

Asplenium. In this *genus* the fructifications are in oblique right lines on the disk of the leaves, which are either simple, pinnatifid, pinnated, or decomposite. Linnæus enumerates 28 species, of which only eight have been found on this island. Of the *A. scolopendrium* Curtis has given a good engraving. These several species are in English called Spleenworts, with some epithet to distinguish them one from another.

Polypodium. Fructifications in roundish spots on the disk of the leaf, in lines parallel to the nerve. We have 14 *species* of this *genus.* There are in all 78. The leaves are variously pinnated. In the *Flora Londinensis* you will find a plate of the *P. vulgare*, Common Polypody.

Adiantum. Seeds in oval spots in the curled extremities of the leaves. Of this *species* there are 27 *genera*, of which only the *A. capillus Veneris*, True Maidenhair, is a native of Britain. It has been found on Barry island, Glamorganshire, and on the isle of Arran in Scotland.

Tri-

Tricomanes. Fructification solitary, terminated by a ftyle like a briftle, on the very edge of the leaf. Of the 13 genera defcribed by Linnæus, we have but two, viz. *T. pyxidiferum*, and *T. tunbrigenfe*. They have both been found in various parts of the kingdom on moift rocks.

Pilularia. Male flowers in a line, like duft, on the under fide of the leaf. Females at the root globular, quadrilocular, containing many feeds. Of this there is but one fpecies, the *globulifera*, Pepper-grafs It creeps along the ground like a mat. The leaves are three or four inches high, and the capfules are like pepper-corns. It is found in places that have been overflowed during the winter.

Ifoetes. Male flower, *antheræ* at the bafe of the inner leaves. Females, *capfula* bilocular, at the bafe of the external leaves. There are of this *genus* but two *fpecies*, one of which has been found at the bottom of fome lakes in Wales and in Scotland. Its fpecific appellation is *lacuftris*, Quilwort. The leaves are jointed, fubulate, and about four or five inches long.

Thefe

Thefe eleven genera comprehend all the Britifh Ferns, or rather let us call them *Filices:* many of them have no refemblance to what we mean by Ferns. The next Order of this Clafs is the *Moffes,* of which Linnæus makes eleven *genera:* nine of them are indigenous with us, *viz.*

Musci, faid to be derived from μοσχος, *vitulus,* a calf, a heifer, a young fhoot, or any thing young. With what propriety, if fuch be the derivation, this fecond Order of the Clafs *Cryptogamia* is thus entitled, I do not underftand: however, we tranflate it *Moffes.* It comprehends thofe plants which have *antheræ* without *filamenta;* whofe female flowers have no *piftillum,* and whofe feed is a naked *corculum.*

Lycopodium, Club-mofs: *antheræ* bivalve, feffile; *calyptra* none. Of the 29 fpecies of Linnæus, we have no more than fix, for a defcription of which I refer you to your *Synopfis;* and, if you have an inclination to be more minutely informed, confult Lightfoot's *Flora Scotica.*

Sphagnum. Bog-mofs: *antheræ* operculate, mouth not bearded. No *calyptra.* There

are

are but three fpecies of this genus, all which are natives of Britain. Of the fpecies *paluſtre*, Linnæus, in his *Flora Lapponica*, tells us, that the Lapland matrons, having dried it, will make a moſt comfortable cradle-bed of it for their infants.

Phaſcum. No *operculum*; no beard: *calyptra* minute. We have, in this kingdom, but three *fpecies* of this *genus*. There are five in all. The generic charaĉter, of Linnæus, even in Murray's laſt edition of the *Syſtema Vegetabilium*, is *anthera operculata*; *ore ciliata*: but Curtis is poſitive that there is no *operculum*, and that the mouth is beardlefs. Of the *Phaſcum acaulon* and *fubulatum* you may fee a very good engraving in the *Flora Londinenſis*.

Fontinalis, Water Mofs: *anthera* operculate; *calyptra* feſſile, inclofed in a *perichætium*. There are but four *fpecies* of this *genus*, which are all natives here: one of thefe Linnæus calls *antipyretica*, becaufe the Swediſh peafants ſtuff it in between the woodwork of their chimneys, to prevent their taking fire. We call it Greater Water-mofs.

Splach-

Splachnum: anthera on a large coloured *apophysis: calyptra* caducous. Female ftar on a feparate individual. Of this, Linnæus has fix fpecies, but two of which are Britifh.

Polytrichum: anthera operculate, on a fmall *apophysis: calyptra* villous. Female ftar in a diftinct individual. The five *fpecies* of this *genus* are indigenous here. If you be defirous of an intimate acquaintance with the *fubrotundum*, confult the *Flora Londinenfis*.

Mnium: anthera operculate: *calyptra* fmooth: Female, a naked bulb, frequently on a feparate ftem. There are twenty *fpecies* of this *genus*, of which we have thirteen. Nine of thefe you will find accurately engraved and defcribed by *Curtis*.

Bryum: anthera operculate: *calyptra* fmooth: a filament from the terminal tubercle. Of thefe there are thirty-feven fpecies in the laft edition of the *Syftema Vegetabilium*: Hudfon had augmented them to forty-five, in this kingdom only. They were fufficiently numerous already. In the *Flora Londinenfis* you will find excellent engravings of nine *fpecies*.

Hypnum.

Hypnum. Differs from the two laſt genera only, in a lateral filament from the *pe-richætium.* Of this genus there are fifty *ſpecies,* about forty of which have been found in Britain. Curtis has three of them.

In Lightfoot's *Flora Scotica,* at the concluſion of this laſt Order of the *Cryptogamia,* you will find ſome moral and very rational reflections on the uſe and importance of Moſſes.

ALGÆ. *Alga,* you know, is a claſſical word for Sea-weeds indiſcriminately. Linnæus adopts it for the title of his third Order of the Claſs *Cryptogamia,* comprehending thoſe plants whoſe roots, ſtem and leaves are all in one. Of theſe there are twelve *genera, viz.*

Jungermannia: Male, pedunculate, naked; *antheræ* quadrivalve. Female, ſeſſile, naked, feeds roundiſh. We have thirty *ſpecies* of this *genus.* There is a good engraving of the *J. complanata* in Curtis.
Targionia: Calyx bivalve, including a globe. Of this there is but one ſpecies, called *Hypophylla,* or Vetch *Targionia.*

 Mar-

Marchantia: Male, *calyx* peltate, covered beneath by monopetalous corollæ; antheræ multifid. Female, calyx feffile, campanulate, polyfpermous. There are feven fpecies of this genus, four of which are Britifh.

Blafia: Calyx cylindrical, filled with feed. Of this there is but one fpecies, called *pufilla*.

Riccia: No calyx; no corolla; antheræ cylindrical, feffile, on the germen. Of thefe there are five, all which have been found in this kingdom.

Anthoceros: Male, *calyx* feffile, truncated entire. Female, *calyx* fexpartite, feeds three.

Lichen, Archel, or Liverwort. Male, *receptaculum fubrotundum, planiufculum.* Female, *farina foliis adfperfis.* Of this *genus* Linnæus has no lefs than a hundred and thirty, about a hundred of which are Britifh. In the *Flora Cantabrigienfis* you will find engravings of three curious fpecies of thefe Lichens, which will give you an idea of the general appearance of thefe plants.

Tremella. A mere gelly: Linnæus has eleven fpecies: five have been defcribed in this kingdom.

Fucus.

Fucus. Male, veficles interwoven with hairs.
Females, veficles full of gelatinous matter. There are fifty-eight fpecies, above
forty of which are found on our coafts.
In the *Flora Scotica* you will find plates
of fix different fpecies of thefe *Fuci,*
which will give you a fufficient idea of
the *habitus* of this *genus.*

Ulva. Laver. Fructification in a diaphanous
membrane. Of the fourteen fpecies of
Ulva, ten are found on our coaft.

Conferva. Fructifications tubular, unequal,
difperfed, on long capillary fibres, either
feffile or floating. Of thefe we have
twenty-nine fpecies.

Byffus. Simple down or powder. Of thefe
we have eleven fpecies.

FUNGI. This Order includes every vegetable of the Fungus or Mufhroom kind.

Agaricus. Linnæus's characteriftic of this
genus is—*Fungus horizontalis, fubtus la-
mellofus.* He might with as much propriety have called a tree, whofe branches
are horizontal, *planta horizontalis.* In
fact there is nothing in this *genus* ho-

 rizontal,

rizontal, except the *pileus* or hat, and that is more frequently conical. The common efculent Mufhroom and every other fungus of that appearance are called Agarics. In the laft edition of the *Syftema Vegetabilium*, there are thirty-nine *fpecies*. Mr. Relhan has defcribed fifty in this county only. Curtis has defcribed and delineated twelve *fpecies*, and in the *Flora Scotica*, you will find a minute defcription of twenty-three.

Boletus. Fungus horizontalis; fubtus porofus. According to this definition, the only difference between this *genus* and the laft, is in there being pores inftead of lamellæ or gills. Some of thefe are with and others without ftems. In the *Flora Londinenfis* you will find a good engraving of a very fingular fpecies of Boletus, which Curtis accidentally met with in the year 1780, and which from its fine polifh he calls *Boletus lucidus*, Lacquered *Boletus*. Linnæus enumerates twenty-one *fpecies*.

Hydnum. Fungus horizontalis, fubtus echinatus. Here again the only diftinction is in the prickles underneath. Linnæus has

five

five species, three of which have been found on this island. Of the *Hydnum aurifcalpium*, there is a plate in *Curtis*.

Phallus. Fungus fupra reticulatus, fubtus lævis. Of this genus Linnæus has three species, one of which is the efculent Morel. Other Botanifts have added a fourth, which they call *caninus:* of this and the *impudicus*, you will fee good engravings in *Curtis*.

Clathrus. Fungus fubrotundus, cancellatus. Of this genus Linnæus has but four species. Hudfon has eight; Relhan four.

Helvella. Fungus turbinatus. Of thefe Linnæus has two species; Hudfon three; Relhan four.

Peziza. Campanulatus, feffilis. Of this genus, Linnæus has eleven *species*; Hudfon fifteen; Relhan thirteen.

Clavaria. Fungus, lævis, oblongus, of which Linnæus has thirteen species, about half of which have been found in Britain.

Lycoperdon. Fungus fubrotundus, feminibus farinaceis repletus. This *genus* includes Truffles and Puff-balls.

Mucor. Mould. Veficles on pedicles. Of this Linnæus has fifteen species.

I have

I have thus endeavoured to give you a fketch of this infinite Clafs of vegetable productions, called *Cryptogamia*. By running your eye over the characters of the Orders and *genera*, you will acquire a general knowledge of the principles of this concealed part of the Linnæan Syftem; and with this general knowledge you may reft fatisfied. If at any time, in future, you fhould happen to have no better employment than microfcopical amufements, the *Cryptogamia* will afford you much entertainment. And now, I fancy, we may fay with Virgil

Claudite jam rivos, pueri, fat prata biberunt.

Vale.

INDEX

INDEX I.

Beau-

C.

Inti-

Pofi-

Sea,

Ullyffes,

I N D E X. II.

B O T A N I C A L.

Bed-

B

C

Cicely,

Larkfpur

Sage,

Thistle,

E R R A T A.

Page 3. line 11. for *Arithmatician*, read *Arithmetician*. P. 20.
l. 2. for *diferemination*, read *diferimination*. P. 128. l. 15.
for *inquifitely*, read *inquifitively*. P. 136. l. 26. for *pilate*,
read *pilot*. P. 137. l. 7. for *pilate*, read *pilot*. P. 139.
l. 25. *Ullyffes*, read *Ulyffes*. P. 128. l. ult. for *turned*, read
tuned. P. 218. l. 8. for *Salvitur*, read *Solvitur*. P. 222.
l. 9. after *founded*, read *on*. P. 227. l. 23. for PALYADEL-
PHIA, read POLYADELPHIA. P. 258. l. 24. for *Vegetabilum*, read *Vegetabilium*. P. 273. l. 13. for *macalatum*, read
maculatum. P. 274. l. 15. for *rebentem*, read *rubentem*.
P. 277. l. 23. for *with*, read *without*. P. 286. l. 26. for
turbular, read *tubular*. P. 301. l. 15. after *barley*, read *and*.
P. 304. l. 13. for *with*, read *without*. P. 306. l. 2. for
turbular, read *tubular*. P. 341. in the margin, for *Spiræa*
read *Epilobium*.